WINNING
AT HALTER

BY DENNY HASSETT

WITH LYNDA BLOOM LAYNE

Due to time lags between the gathering and publishing of information, typographic gremlins, and other circumstances involved when dealing with large volumes of data, neither the author nor the publisher can guarantee complete accuracy of the information presented in this book. The author and publisher welcome corrections, updates and additions. The purpose of this book is to educate and entertain, not to offer legal or other professional advice. Neither the publisher nor the author accepts any responsibility for any decisions or actions or their consequences taken as a result of the information presented in this book.

For information:
Breakthrough Publications, Inc.
www.booksonhorses.com

ISBN: 0-914327-90-9

07 06 05 04 03   9 8 7 6 5 4 3 2 1

Photographs by Lynda Bloom Layne, except where noted

Edited by Audrey Pavia

Book interior designed by Kraus & Associates

Illustrations by Pam Tanzey

Cover: A Beter Offer
1997 AQHA Stallion
owned by Quiet Meadow Quarter Horse Ranch, Susan & Eldon Stevenson & Dale Borders, Chattaroy, Washington. Fitted and shown by Laurie Takoff, Laurian Quarter Horses, Kelowna, BC Canada.

Photograph by Dan Stuttgart

Impreso por Imprelibros S.A.
Impreso en Colombia – Printed in Colombia

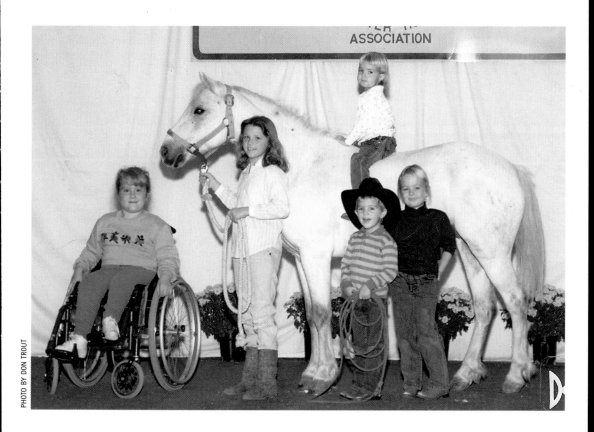

PHOTO BY DON TROUT

In loving memory

of our true competitor,

Amber Dawn Coleman

1/16/81 – 12/15/99

Several years ago, while still living in California, I was in my third decade of showing western halter horses. I was still searching for new and effective ways to fit and show my horses, since I did all the work myself.

One day I saw a clinic on halter horses by a trainer at the American Quarter Horse Congress. I digested every word of that trainer's advice. Before long, my Paints and Quarter Horses were looking better and winning bigger. I became a big fan of the man who did that clinic.

he had a good one. He knew that if everything went right as this colt grew, someday this horse would have a shot at the top. It all boiled down to Mother Nature doing her part, with Denny putting in the hard work, consistency and dedication it takes to fit a champion.

That's what I learned working with Denny. As you read this book, you'll see how a regular routine produces results. You'll discover that you can't sit in your house in front of an air conditioner on a blistering summer day and say, "Aw, shucks. It's too hot to rub on that horse. I'll just stay in here where I'm comfortable."

When preparing a horse for halter competition, you can't take shortcuts with your grooming, fitting or feeding programs. Fitting a halter horse is hard work, but will also be one of the most rewarding experiences you'll ever have.

During the months I spent working with Denny, and the subsequent years I researched for this book, each time I walked down the aisleway of Denny's barn and saw World and Congress Champions and Reserve Champions like GQ Eclipse, his sire Mister. GQ, Gee Que Silhouette, Pure Play, River City Renegade and Classical Conclusion, I thought about how wonderful it was just to be in their presence. Every time I worked, rubbed or rinsed one of them, I picked up more knowledge about what it takes to produce a winner in the Hassett way.

I loved learning the tricks of the trade from Denny Hassett. So will you.

— *Lynda Bloom Layne*

That trainer was Denny Hassett.

After moving to Kansas, I was lucky enough to meet Denny and his wife, Dana. I felt even luckier when they bought a facility just miles away from my house. I was able to work with them and the horses in their barn, gaining hands-on experience that would ultimately help me put this book together. Denny's enthusiasm and love for his work are contagious.

Denny is one of those positive, upbeat people who knows he's darned lucky to be spending his life doing what he loves. Every win in the show pen is as exciting for him as the first. Some are even sweeter.

At one American Quarter Horse Association World Show, I watched Denny balance that big World Champion trophy on one arm as he led the yearling stallion Pure Play out of the arena. Denny's eyes sparkled and a wide grin lit up his face. He walked to where Dana was standing, glanced at the young stallion, then to Dana and said, "I told you—he had what takes to be World Champion."

Denny had picked Pure Play out of the pack when the colt was 7 days old. His finely tuned horseman's eye—along with his heart—told him

The thrill of putting a halter horse on a fitting program and watching him bloom, peak and then win The Big One is an absolutely phenomenal experience.

Our program focuses on aiming for the World shows with our Quarter Horses and Paints. It's what we work for all year long.

Maybe your program doesn't have such high aspirations. Perhaps you enjoy competing at weekend shows or you aim for a state fair or futurity to wrap up your year. Every level of competition offers a wonderful experience, no matter what your goal.

The most important advice I can offer is to choose a horse that will make you competitive in your chosen level of competition. Then, work hard at reaching your goal. There are no shortcuts in fitting halter horses. Every moment you invest pays off in big dividends.

This book will show you how we work toward our goals. It will offer you the how's and why's of producing a halter horse that dazzles a judge. My wife, Dana, and I hope you will experience all the joys we have in our fitting and showing of more than 45 World and Reserve World champions.

We're with you all the way!

— *Denny Hassett*

Choosing a
Halter Prospect

Before you set out to choose a halter prospect, visualize the quality

of the horses you will show against. Not everyone is headed for the

World Show or Quarter Horse Congress. You might only be inter-

ested in leading your halter horse at small weekend or 4-H shows.

Whatever your program, you need a horse that will fit into it. If you

have already been competing at the level you are aiming at, or have

watched some classes, you have a pretty good idea of the quality

you need in a horse in order to do well.

Looking at Raw Material

In the very end of his weanling year, GQ Eclipse showed us a wonderful overall picture, from the gorgeous head and neck, to the sloped shoulder, long wither, straight topline and good loin. You can see the flair in his hip and forearm and how his legs set on nicely. He was still unshown when these photos were taken and had only been in our fitting program for two weeks. You're looking at "raw material" here. Here's a breakdown:

a His long neck is clean and flat from his shoulder to his poll. The bottom of his neck tapers up into a fine, tight throatlatch.

b He has a great slope to his shoulder and a long wither.

c His neck ties in high to his chest.

d He has a nice line from his buttocks to his hocks.

e He has the right slope from his tail set to his stifle.

f He has a lot of depth from the stifle to the back of the buttocks. Anytime you have a horse with this good depth you'll have one that also has a lot of croup.

g-h The base of his stifle is wider than the top of his hip. He has a lot of pop and flair.

i This colt also has a lot of inside gaskin.

j You can easily see his shoulder points.

k His forearm already has pop and flair. His legs set out well on his shoulders.

l He has a tremendous deep "V" in his chest.

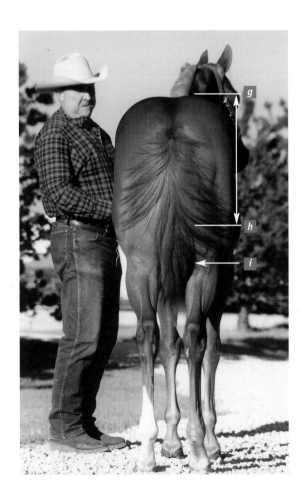

Eclipse has a beautiful head and eye.

Keep in mind that many of the conformation traits we are about to discuss are pluses. Just because a horse doesn't have all the extras doesn't mean he isn't a good individual. Not all horses have ideal conformation. If the best horse in a class has, say, one foot that turns out, or a little crest in his neck that wont sweat down, he could still win if he's the best horse in the class and presents the finest overall picture.

Maybe your horse doesn't have a monstrous hind leg and a big, heavy stifle, but he's still pretty and well balanced. He might still have the competitive edge from that standpoint. After all, the horses behind him might not have all that either, and could have four or five faults to your horse's one. Don't think that because your horse isn't perfect that he shouldn't be shown or that you should get rid of him. If he's a good individual overall, give him the benefit of the doubt.

Look for an individual that can win for you one day and if you get beat a time or two after that, can come back and win another one later. We would all like to lead a horse that wins every time, but that doesn't always happen. What we need to focus on is a horse that is competitive within our level of competition.

Looking at Foals

At the beginning of the day, horses are fresh and their true conformation is better represented.

Their backs are straight, and their legs are well under them. But, after a day of working and playing, the back won't appear as strong and will often have a saggy appearance. The hocks, which were straight down under the horse, will often stick out behind. Overall, the horse won't look as firm. If you're sizing up a prospect, you don't get the full effect of his true assets if you view him when he's tired.

I've gone to some places to look at horses and have gotten the babies up at daybreak. I just walk out into the pasture where they have been down all night. If a baby gets up and his back is straight, and his legs and hocks are good, I can just about bet that is the way he will be down the road. But if he gets up and he is cocking over in his front ankles or he is bad in his hocks, I'm skeptical. I can't say for sure he will stay that way, but I will put off my decision and look at him again in 30 days or more.

Where do I find babies? Breeders ask me to come look at their foals. Or I might be taking a mare in to breed to one of their stallions and will always take time to look at the babies. If I see 10 or 15 foals by the time I leave the place, I have a pretty good idea of what I want and like.

Still, babies change back and forth so much that in most cases, I don't make an immediate decision. The foal I like best at 30 days I might not like later, and vice versa. I like to see babies

What You Hope They Become

1 This is GQ Eclipse as a 3-year-old. You can see the tremendous maturity that has taken place, and how his good points just got better.

2 You can see how maturity has built on the basics that were there when Eclipse was a weanling. This is the modern look.

3 Notice the pop and flair in his gaskin and forearm

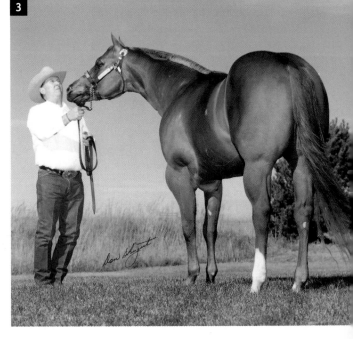

when they are first born, then again in 30 days and then check them out the next time when they are around 3 months old. Then, 30 days after they are taken from their mothers, I like to see how they have made it through the hard times of weaning. A lot of babies look good on their mothers, but when you take them off, they regress and won't snap back fast enough to get ready for fall futurities. The ones who are going to make it will slack off for a week or two, then start coming back, and just get better and better. Normally, they are the ones that have the quality to be futurity babies. They look great 30 to 45 days after weaning.

Though I check the babies out part by part, I'm looking at how these individual pieces are presented in an overall picture. And, looking at a baby, I try to visualize what he will look like four, five or six months down the road. This isn't always possible to predict, because babies change so much. But usually, if the horse is going to be a good baby, he will be correct in his legs; will have some forearm sticking out; and will have some V in his chest. His loin and hip will also be good.

Let's look at those parts and how they tie in to produce that nice overall picture.

A pretty head is, of course, a real attention-getter. River City Renegade, who was an AQHA two-time World Champion, had that big, bulge eye when he was born, and it stayed that way. For many horses this area goes through a lot of changes. I've seen babies that weren't real good-headed, but grew into their heads as yearlings or 2-year-olds and looked great. I've also seen it go the other way.

A nice neck is certainly an asset to any halter horse. I like to see a baby with a long neck that is somewhat flat. In fact, when they are babies, they can be just a hair low in the neck from the wither, and will normally fill in later. If you take a horse that has an arch in his neck as a baby, and has a wide hair line at the top of his neck (for the mane), as he gets older, you are going to be fighting a crest. If you get him too heavy, it will go right to that neck. If you have a horse with a real thin, fine hair line and just a little arch, you won't have nearly as much crest in the neck later.

It's important that the neck tie in nicely underneath to the chest. Ideally, the neck ties in high and moves to a pretty, tapered throatlatch. Even if a horse is not real long necked, if the

This closeup shows the pop and flair on the forearm of a 2-year-old filly.

neck he has fits him right, it will appear longer than it is. But, take a horse with the same length of neck that is set on 3 or 4 inches too deep into the chest, and his neck will look short.

If a horse ties in too deep, this will visually take away from his front end. He can be a horse with a pretty V-chest, but if the neck ties in clear down towards that V, it distracts from the nice front end.

Most babies will go through growth and weight changes while on their mothers. This will sometimes affect their hocks. They will seem long and thin one day, then short and fat the next. This is one reason it's a good idea to look at a prospect over several months to see if he will change.

River City Renegade was an exception to this rule. Proportionately, his neck was as long when he was a baby as it was when he was mature. He never went through that baby stage where his neck appeared short and fat. If you are looking at a horse that is going through that stage, give him time and then check him out again.

When the necks stretch out again, look for a nice tie-in; that is the way that neck fits into the chest and at the shoulder. If a horse has a nice sloped shoulder, his withers will carry way back. If his shoulder is straight, he will have a shorter wither.

A straight topline and strong loin are real pluses for a halter horse, but sometimes when you are looking at babies, it's a hard trait to judge. Often, when a baby is on a growth spurt, his croup shoots up higher than his withers for a period of time. A well-balanced baby won't get too out of whack when he's growing, but he will show some difference. Others will have a few inches difference in the front and back. To check to see if a baby will balance out, look at his legs.

Check the difference in the front and back cannon bones. The hocks are, of course, going to be higher than the knees, but if the difference in length of those front and back cannon bones is extreme when a baby is 2 or 3 weeks old, he may be the type that stays out of balance and never evens out. In other words, his back cannon bones are excessively long and his fronts very short. His croup is much higher than his withers and he looks like he's traveling downhill. He might mature with a 4- to 5-inch difference in front and back.

While you are looking at the legs, think about how they are made. If you're looking at a real young baby who was big and cramped up inside his mother, it's going to take him some time to straighten out. Ideally, you want to see a horse whose pastern is at the same angle as his shoulder. If a baby has very long pasterns and is standing way down on them—giving a coon-footed appearance—you will want to see if he comes back up to a more normal slope. Some will strengthen up with time. If he's out of balance and downhill now, when he comes up on those front legs, he might level out more on his topline.

Other babies have the opposite problem and are real upright and steep in the pastern. Hopefully, the tendons will stretch down as the baby grows and he will show a more normal slope. Some will never have enough tendon stretch to come down.

Check the baby's knees. A judge will nail him if he has pronounced offset or calf knees. I think a calf knee (which bends back like an over-extension) is a bigger problem than one that is a little over at the knees.

One thing to realize with babies is that since their legs are so long at birth, when they start to attempt to graze and straddle their front feet out to the sides, they wear off the insides of their hooves. He might appear crooked-legged, but the real problem is that the baby needs his hooves trimmed or rasped off level. (Our farrier, Richard Clower, explains this in Chapter 9.

I've seen babies change a lot in their hocks, but the rule of thumb is that you want those hocks to line up with the buttock and not stick way out behind. If a colt is a little out behind, he might straighten up. If you can, look at the baby's sire and dam to see if they are good in the hocks. If they are, it could be an indication that the baby might improve.

When a foal is a very young baby, you can see if he is going to have a well-sloped shoulder angle and a nice, deep heart girth. These are the ideals. The shoulder structure is not going to change as the baby gets older, but if he is currently a little shallow in the rear, he might develop this later. He could just be a slow developer.

Though this doesn't have a huge bearing on my choice, I look at the tail set as part of the overall picture. I don't like a real flat croup with a tail that sticks out. Nor do I like one that is so steep it looks like a pitch roof. I like a medium croup with a lot of length.

When sizing up the hip, stifle and gaskin area from the back, I like to see the stifle as wide or wider than the base of the hip. Ideally, there is a lot of pop and flair in the stifle. When you look at the gaskin, you hope for the inside leg to be pretty near as adequate as the outside. You don't always get this. It's just a plus.

Looking at the hip and stifle from the side, I don't like to see the horse's hip drop straight down from the tail set to the gaskin. There should be some flair, getting deep and bigger as it comes down, instead of coming down flat. This is another plus. You don't discount a horse for not having it. It's just a bonus if he does.

Looking at Yearlings

Most of what I've said about choosing weanlings applies to yearlings as well. You should look for overall correctness and balance in a horse of any age. When sizing up a yearling, you are looking for all of that in a bigger version. If you are choosing one at the end of his weanling year or the first of his yearling year, by then you will have seen the weanling classes and know which horses you will be showing against as yearlings.

Size will enter the overall picture here. I'm not saying the prospect has to be huge, but the one you choose should be of adequate size and quality to compete against what is being shown in your chosen level of competition.

I'm not stressing strictly size here. Some people ask why young halter horses have to be so big. The main point is that you hope for balance and quality, but if you have two horses out there that are equal in these points, but one is 14.3 hands and the other is 15.3, the judge is going to choose the bigger horse.

When you choose one to start with at the first of his yearling year, hope that as the year progresses, he will "body up" and turn into as great an individual as you thought he would. With halter horses, you are always at the mercy of Mother Nature.

Looking at 2-Year-Olds and Beyond

Two-year-olds must have more substance at this age because lack of bulk will start to hurt them in the show pen. Balance is also still extremely important. Plus, the bulk in front and back must match. Do the parts look like they belong to the same horse?

Your 2-year-old might have a lot of mass and muscle in the front end and be real deep in the heart-girth. The neck might tie in high and nice at the chest. Everything up front looks good, but when you go to the back, you don't have as much mass, not much pop and flair to the gaskin, and maybe something lacking in the stifle area. The

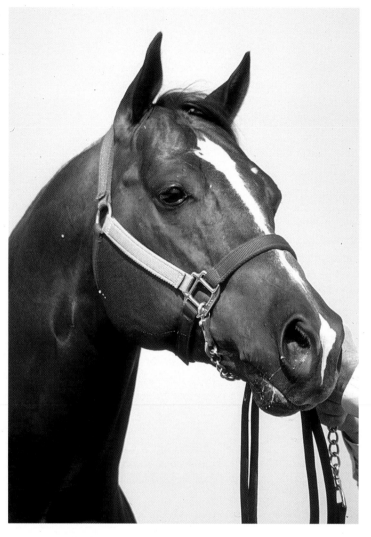

ing front or back ends, but I think a horse needs both the great front and back end and a dynamite profile. For instance, if that horse with the great front and back is coarse through the head and neck, and soft in the middle with a sagging topline, he's just not going to present a great profile.

The last decade has seen profile horses winning big. So when you choose a prospect of any age, look at the overall picture. Stand off to the side of that horse and see if he has a super nice profile along with balance and mass.

hip doesn't come way out and down. The front end looks like it belongs to one horse and the back end to another. A horse like this just doesn't balance up.

As young horses mature with age, they also have to mature in body. Three-year-olds ideally carry more bulk and mass than younger horses. And when horses graduate into the aged classes, they really need that bulk. Incidentally, this isn't the bulk from the days of old in the halter pen, when it was common to see what was referred to as the "bulldog look." Instead, it's bulk with a modern look, which means the horse has defined muscle but also has "stretch."

What is the modern look? It's smooth and pretty, especially through the head and neck, but the horse still has a lot of muscle. The overall profile and pretty look, along with balance, will win more than it will with a horse that is just heavily made and has all the muscle and gristle in the world, but no refinement. There are many horses out there that can win on their outstand-

Housing the
Halter Horse

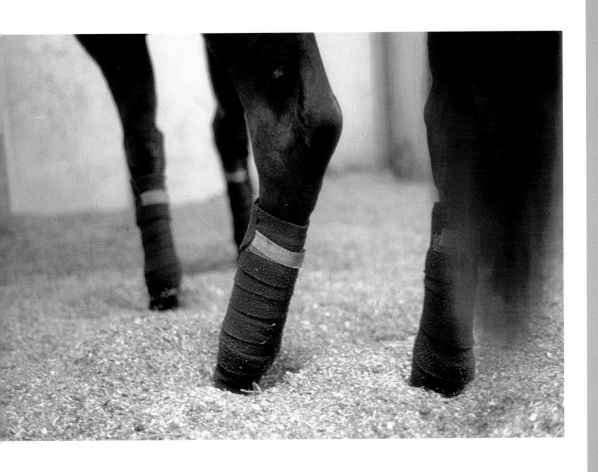

When it comes to housing, it's important to provide your halter horse with a clean, safe, draft-free and well-ventilated environment. Even if you don't have a big fancy barn, giving your horse everything he needs is a priority.

Because Kansas winters are harsh, we keep a small overhead 7,000 BTU heater mounted on the north wall of our barn. Our aim is to maintain the entire show barn at a constant 68 degrees during the colder months. Our horses wear one nylon sheet during this time. If we wanted to use heavy blankets, we could keep the barn temperature cooler. But the 68-degrees-and-sheet combination works well for us. This is what we do to produce great hair coats.

In other parts of the country where winters are milder, heated barns are not a necessity. Under these conditions, some horses keep nice coats by having sheets or blankets put on to correspond with the need, based on the barn temperature.

If you do decide to heat your barn, I suggest you speak with a heating specialist so you know what safety precautions to take as far as ventilation and exhaust. And think carefully about where you want to set that thermostat, and coordinate it with what your horses will wear. Heavy blankets equal cooler temperatures, and lightweight sheets equal warmer temperatures.

Especially in states like Kansas where it is often very cold at night and warm in the daytime, and you have no way to heat your barn, you will have to use heavy blankets and a hood at night. Then, by about 9 a.m. when it starts to warm up, feel under the blanket to see if the horse is sweaty. If he feels just a little tacky, he's fine. But if he is sweating, pull the blanket off and put one on that is not as heavy. You may have to switch to an even lighter weight blanket later in the day, then go back to the heavies at night. It's a good idea to keep three weights of blankets on hand.

In the winter, any barn that is closed up will have problems with ammonia fumes coming from urine in the stalls. We have an exhaust fan that automatically kicks on when the humidity in the barn gets above 50 percent. The fan clears and freshens the air. Another big victory in the ammonia smell war is realized through regular stall cleaning.

We have thick rubber mats covering the concrete floors of our stalls. Because the concrete is solid and is slightly sloped, urine moves forward to the stall front, allowing wet shavings to easily be pulled out. We never leave any urine on those mats, and wet shavings come out every day.

We bed just as deep with the concrete and mats as we did when we had a barn with dirt floors covered with mats. Our shavings come in 8-cubic-feet bags, and we use from 12 to 14 bags per stall when we bed fresh. Once a week, we

Our stalls have grilled fronts and doors. In the summer, we mount box fans on the stall grills with bungee cords.

replace the amount of shavings we estimate were removed in the daily cleanings, which is usually three to four bags.

Each day, we turn all the shavings in the stall, flipping them over with a fork, picking out the wet areas and manure. We turn the center first, then throw the shavings closest to the walls into the middle, leveling it like a mesa. This leaves the shavings somewhat banked up, but not too high in the center since the horses might get cast.

As the horses walk around in their stalls, they eventually spread much of the center shavings back toward the walls. For the most part, our method keeps them from walking a hole in the shavings in the middle of the stall.

In the summer months, we open our south overhead door so the outside air flows through the alleyway. Still, the stalls are pretty warm when the mercury climbs into the high-90 or low-100 degree ranges. To keep the horses comfortable, we put box fans on the stall door grills and mount them with bungee cords. We are very careful not to have an electrical cord where a horse can grab it.

Since we work our horses in the morning, before the heat of the day, we don't turn the fans on until after the horses have been worked,

sweated and rinsed, then dried and rubbed out the final time. The fans go on in the heat of the afternoon and stay on until the barn starts to cool off in the evening.

Some barns are built with windows in the outside stall walls. I don't care for that because often times the air inside the stalls is warmer than the air outside that is blowing in through the window. Cool air hits warm horses and they get snotty noses from it. It is also detrimental to a nice hair coat.

The placement of feeders and waterers in a stall has a lot to do with how safe that stall will be. I don't think you can build something that is 100-percent accident proof. Any time you have an open area like a hay feeder, there is bound to be a horse that has the ingenuity to get a foot caught in it. One way to minimize this possibility is to mount your feeders or waterers in a corner.

Don't forget a light program necessary to keep hair coats slick. Our standard fluorescent shop lights are on a timer that turns them on at 5:30 a.m. and off at 10:30 p.m. With a light program, the hours of darkness are just as important as the hours of light. A horse needs both.

The show-barn part of our set-up consists of 12 portable stalls set inside the metal barn,

which is insulated both in the ceiling and in the outside walls. The sheet metal that lines the stalls is not only easy to keep clean, but is more maintenance-free than wood. Any time you have wood, you'll have horses that chew. At our previous location, where we did have wood stalls, we lined them with metal.

With our portable barn set-up, if one wall does get damaged, we can replace it without having to tear the whole barn apart.

Our barn is equipped with an automatic fly control system, which sprays from an overhead sprinkler-type device. This is especially important in regions like ours where surrounding ranches have a lot of cattle, increasing the fly population. Not only does the absence of flies in the stalls keep the horses less stressed and more comfortable, but those highly desirable full tails are not constantly whipping at flies, which causes hair loss or breakage.

Overall, we like to house our halter horses in a comfortable, pleasant, low-stress environment.

Deworming, Shots and Teeth

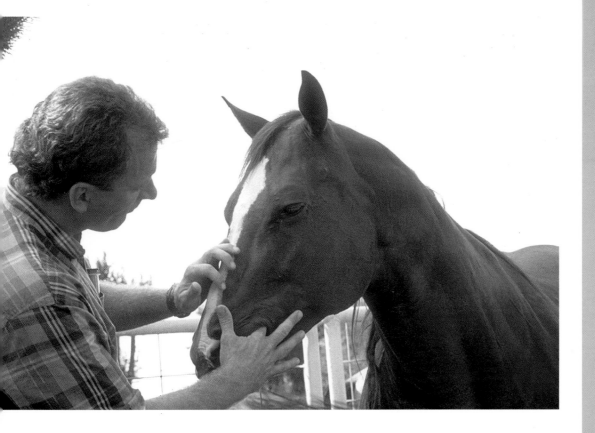

J ames Speer, D.V.M., of Wichita, Kansas, oversees our program of parasite control, vaccinations and teeth floating. I asked him to explain why these elements of equine health care are such an important part of a halter horse fitting program, and how they should be managed. Here is what he had to say.—Denny Hassett

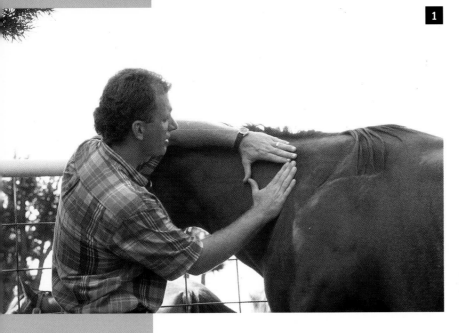

 The neck is also an option as an injection site, if the shot is given in the triangular area James Speer, DVM, is pointing out here.

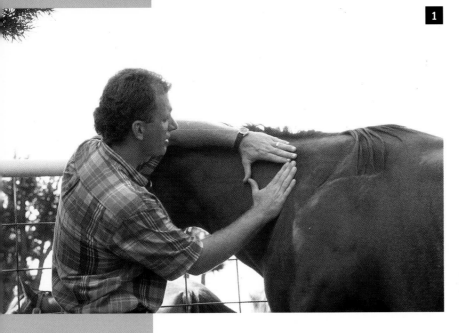 According to Dr. Speer, if you need to administer a vaccination to a horse in the hip, use the deep, heavy muscle area in the back. If you give an injection in the top of the hip, and the horse experiences injection site reaction or forms an abscess, he won't pick up his back leg on that side.

Parasite Control

By James Speer, DVM

Denny wants to keep his horses as parasite free as possible, and I think he does a good job at this. In the halter horse pen, everything has to be perfect. Any parasite challenge could affect the horse's hair coat and feed efficiency. Denny doesn't want the horses in his environment to get to the point where egg laying parasites are producing positive fecal exams. So regular deworming is performed rather than relying on fecal exams.

Even with the most immaculate barn and the most ideal environment—and Denny's set-up is ideal—there can still be parasite transmission as a result of horses being brought in from other environments. When trying to fit a World Champion, the possibility of parasites causing abnormalities in a horse's metabolism are not worth the risk. Denny is very conscientious about parasite management because he knows it is silly not to have control over it. Given the value of these horses, it is easier to address potential problems with a regular program than it is to let parasites become a problem in the first place.

Typically, with Denny's program, we worm every 60 days with Strongid and Panacur (or fenbendazoles) as our primary dewormers. Denny has a minimal number of gasterophilus (bots) in his barn because of the automatic fly system. But since horses do come in from other places and may be infected with them, we worm once a year with a boticide.

Like so many people fitting halter horses, Denny works a lot on young horses that are of an age that makes them susceptible to ascarid infection. Once ascarids infect an environment, they can remain persistent for a considerable period of time. Ascarids can be on walls, on feeders, or on water buckets. This parasite must be controlled in order to achieve optimum feed efficiency and performance.

A variety of situations in a barn like Denny's can result in parasite infection. When horses come in from other environments, they often stay for at least 60 days. If a horse doesn't work out, he goes home and another horse comes in and goes to the same stall. Babies arriving after weaning may have been exposed to parasites by their mothers since strongyles can be passed through the bloodstream. Colts also lick around the perennial region. And when the mare lays down in her environment, she can make contact with the parasite ova and pick them up on her mammary glands. The colt will then ingest them when he nurses.

We worm the mares at Denny's barn 30 days before they foal so they won't be infected with ova or larvae that may be transmitted to the baby. We then worm the foal at 3 months and continue the program every six to eight weeks.

Safe Vaccine Locations

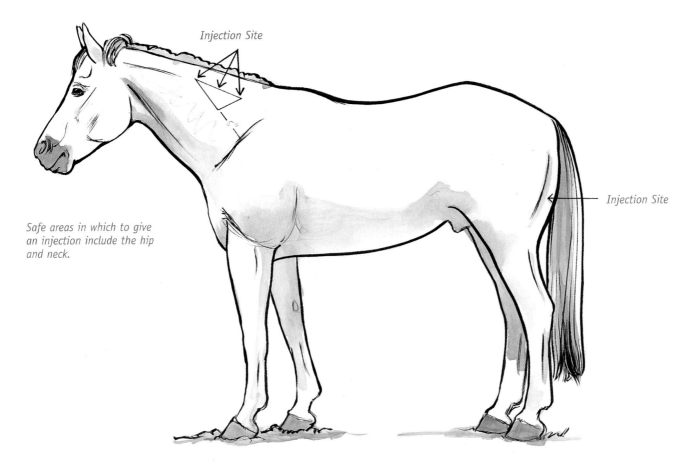

Injection Site

Injection Site

Safe areas in which to give an injection include the hip and neck.

When you are setting up your own program and deciding between tube deworming and paste, look at both sides of the issue. With tube deworming, you are assured of total product delivery. If you choose to paste worm, remember that one tube might not be enough depending on the weight of the horse. It is not uncommon for an aged halter horse to weigh 1,350 to 1,450 pounds, so be sure to dose the horse according to weight.

All of Denny's deworming management is aimed at preventing parasite challenge. Different modes of transmission of parasites, and the transitions resulting from horses coming and going, necessitate the need for a consistent deworming schedule.

Vaccinating

When fitting halter horses, it is mandatory to employ a good heated climate system in the winter. If you keep a steady environment, your horses will maintain their appetites and won't go through the seasonal changes that outside horses experience. The down side to this is that barn

ventilation won't be as ideal as you would like it to be. Consequently, your barn may contain aerosolization of contagious agents brought from various horses coming in from different situations and different parts of the country. You also face this at some shows, especially in the winter, when stabling is closed and heated and a large number of horses from many areas are present in one barn.

Typically, if I have a client who is taking a horse into a barn with a complete climate control environment, I like to give this horse a flu/rhino vaccination three weeks prior to his entering that environment. Then, I will booster him just before he goes to the barn, or just after he has arrived. This does two things: It provides a specific immunity against the flu/rhino virus, and as an immune stimulant, it enhances overall protection.

With babies, the immune system is not as efficient. At 3 months of age, the passive immunity acquired from the mother's colostrum begins to wane. Then, it takes babies until 6 to 12 months of age before they really develop a functional immune system of their own. It is important to provide young horses with vaccines that are going to stimulate their immunities.

All horses need a four-way vaccine once a year, as part of the spring vaccination series. For horses that are being hauled to shows, I recommend that a flu/rhino vaccine be given every 60 to 90 days, minimum.

Regardless of the vaccine you are using, the initial dose should be given, and then be followed by a booster in three to four weeks. Because you are dealing with halter horses, swelling or impairment of movement must be avoided. Be careful about the location where you give the vaccinations as there is always a danger of injection-site reaction.

Regardless of what you are administering to a halter horse, consider giving the injection in the neck or the back of the hip, half-way between where the hip slopes off and starts going in, and the level of the stifle—but no lower. This is good, deep, heavy muscle area with an excellent blood supply. (See diagram on page 27.)

If you give an injection in the top of the hip, and the horse experiences an injection site reaction or forms an abscess, he is not going to pick up his back leg on that side. Localized pain and swelling will indicate a problem. If a horse develops an injection-site reaction, call your veterinarian immediately.

Teeth

Problems with teeth can cause discomfort to your horse while he is chewing, and so can inter-

fere with the efficiency of your feeding program. If your horse is tipping his head to the side or seems to be dropping grain, he may have a problem that needs your veterinarian's attention.

Tooth problems don't just occur in older horses. Babies can also experience sharp edges and won't eat well because the insides of their cheeks are sensitive. It is not difficult to float a baby's teeth to remove those sharp edges.

To find out if a horse has a tooth problem, do not attempt a dental exam. Instead, evaluate the situation by simply applying a light, steady pressure on the outside of the horse's cheeks, over the molar region. If the teeth are sharp, the horse will open his mouth and move away from the pressure. If this happens, arrange to have your veterinarian float the horse's teeth to make him more comfortable.

Long hooks on a horse's teeth will prevent good grinding action on grain. A good halter horse trainer does not allow his horses to get to this point.

Every horse in Denny's barn has its teeth checked at least twice a year and then floated as indicated. In 2- to 5-year-old horses, we also look for problems with erupting permanent teeth. Incisors don't cause problems, but retained caps on molars will. If the horse is showing any discomfort, we will remove the caps in order to keep feed efficiency as high as we can, and to prevent disturbances in appetite.

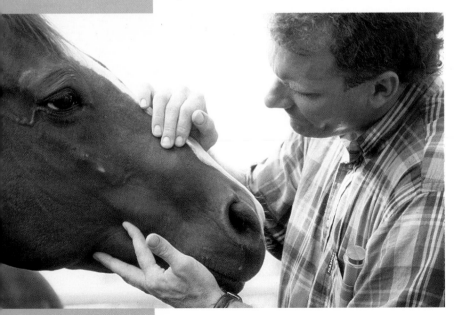

An Overview of Our Feeding Program

When fitting halter horses, a good feeding program is of the utmost importance. We feed our halter horses to produce hardness of body rather than just fat, heavy bulk. We do this by feeding more of a grain ratio than a hay ration. Compare it to buying beef out of the feed yard. If the cattle are grain fed, the quality and muscling are far superior to the cattle that are fed only hay.

We try to feed just enough alfalfa hay to supply the roughage required to ward off colic and other digestion problems. It sometimes requires tearing a flake in half to get this amount. In general, by weight, the average we give an adult horse is probably less than 3 ½ to 4 pounds per feeding.

In most cases, when we want to increase weight, we do so by adding grain and leaving the hay ration the same. The exception to this is the very hard keeper that does not respond to the added grain. If we know that this is the kind of horse who won't get soggy—that is develop a belly—we will increase his hay some, but we won't free-choice feed him. We are careful about this because I'm a firm believer that in most cases, if you feed too much hay, you take away from the hard definition and put on belly.

If a horse needs his body weight reduced, we cut back on both hay and grain, still keeping the grain as the biggest part of the feeding program.

All this centers around peaking a horse, and with our program, we are focused on peaking for the World Show. You can't hold a horse at peak for a very long time.

What exactly is peak? This is when a horse is everything you want him to be. His weight is just right. His hair coat is perfect. His muscling is really developed. You don't really know how long you can hold him there because a horse is prone to go up and down.

For example, we had a 2-year-old stallion that peaked four weeks before the World. I knew I couldn't hold him in that condition for 30 days and that if I kept feeding him the same way, he would go over the desired weight. Since he was the kind of horse that you could fill up in a matter of days (because he was such a good eater), I was able to cut him back on feed. I took away about ⅓ scoop of oats and a little hay. This just

Beware Of Blister Beetles

A good reason to rely on your county extension agent for nutritional advice is to find out if deadly blister beetles are a problem in your part of the country.

When I first moved from California to Kansas, I was confronted with a good news-bad news situation. Beautiful alfalfa could be bought for a fraction of California prices, but if that beautiful hay contained blister beetles, I could wind up with fat, shiny, dead horses. When I was in Kansas, I was careful to purchase alfalfa from reputable dealers who knew I was feeding it to horses.

According to a Kansas State University (KSU) Cooperative Extension Service publication titled *Blister Beetles in Alfalfa*, "Blister beetles can be crushed and killed as alfalfa is swathed. When the hay is baled, bodies of dead beetles, which still contain cantharidin, sometimes become incorporated into the bales. Cantharidin may contaminate hay without the beetle bodies being evident if the beetles are squashed during hay making."

The chemical cantharidin is an irritant which is capable of blistering a horse's body tissues, both internal and external. Horses are especially susceptible to blister beetle poisoning, and according to the KSU publication, this poisoning can be fatal.

Second and fourth cuttings of alfalfa have the greatest risk of contamination by blister beetles, but no cutting can be guaranteed absolutely blister-beetle free. The type of equipment used to cut the hay can influence the presence of beetles. Says the KSU publication, "Among those examined were sicklebar mowers, pull-type swathers with conditioning rollers, and various types of self-propelled mowers."

Trying to spot beetles in alfalfa can be next to impossible. Sometimes, only a small area in a field will have a serious beetle infestation. One KSU test found 145 grams of dead blister beetles—enough to kill 29 horses.

The KSU publication states that keeping the beetles alive and healthy would mean they would be able to leave the field. This could minimize alfalfa contamination.

I urge you to speak with your county agent about problems with blister beetles in your area.

—Lynda Bloom Layne

---

leveled him out on his feeding program. Just before the World, I filled him up just a little more and he looked great.

Looked is the key word here.

When you are feeding a halter horse, you want to use how he looks and how much he is working to determine how you should feed him. First, let's examine how he looks, which is based a great deal on what a horse's conformation is like as an individual.

If a horse has a big hip and you want to call attention to it, then you don't want to put so much weight on him that he fills too much in the flank area. If you do, he will put on some belly and that will take the emphasis away from the hip. If his bottom line is up and tight, his big hip will be more pronounced.

A longer bodied horse usually has to carry a little more weight through the barrel to minimize that length of back. But this only works if the horse has a good, strong and straight topline. If he drops off behind his wither and has a weak topline, he won't benefit from that added weight. In other words, if you put more weight on a horse like this, his topline looks weaker—almost saggy.

Let's say you have a horse with the desirable deep heart-girth and a great stifle area. If you add too much weight and it gives him a belly that is full clear back to the flanks, it takes away from his good points. He will look shallow in the heart. If you keep him tight, his heart girth will look deeper because his bottom line comes up toward his flank area. This will also accentuate a good stifle.

Necks also enter the picture when you are determining how to feed each horse. If a horse has a neck that ties in too deep at his chest, added weight on his belly will make his neck look worse. But, if he is a horse whose neck comes out nice and high at the chest, and the neck is long and sets on right, adding weight won't distract from this.

The work program also has a lot to do with how much weight your horse will have. You have to feed in accordance with the way you are working him. If he is just starting his exercise program and isn't working long, but you are giving him all the feed he wants, he will get soggy and fat. The key is to avoid overfeeding. Start him out easy at first on the feed, and as you increase his work, bump up his feed. It might take a while to figure out his needs.

The babies we bring in to our barn have usually been creep fed. We start them out on two

Testing Hay

by Dave Kehler
Kansas State University Extension Agent

Every class of animal has its own nutrient requirements, and it's especially important to realize the different classes of horses. A growing weanling or yearling, especially if he is being fit to show, has higher needs than that of the idle, mature horse.

You can't be a successful horse nutrition manager by just copying someone else's feeding program. You have to understand the reasons behind why the other person chose this program. For instance, Denny feeds oats, which are higher in fiber content and much safer because of their digestibility. With oats, colic is not a great concern. However, oats by themselves are not going to give enough protein and concentrate for some classes of horses, which is why Denny adds a 30 percent protein supplement to bring his overall total to about 14 percent.

Because of content tags on today's commercial grains, it is easy to see what you are feeding. But what if your hay isn't up to par? The National Research Council (NRC) book *Nutrient Requirements of Horses,* lists a number of percentages, such as total digestible nutrients (TDN), mega cals, net energy gain (very important for young, growing horses) and, of course, protein. One listing in the current book shows an average of

$19\frac{1}{2}$ percent protein for alfalfa in early bloom, down to 16 percent in full bloom. If you are feeding a lower protein hay while you are fitting your halter horses, it can hurt your overall program.

There is a relatively easy way to determine the content of your hay. Your extension agent can help you arrange to have a forage sample run. There are actual core samplers that you can drill into a random selection of bales from your load of hay. They look similar to balling guns used for cattle. Basically, you'll want to sample either 10 bales, or 10 percent of your lot. (A lot is all the hay that was baled out of the same field at the same time.)

If you don't have access to a core sampler, just break open your test bales and pull out a handful from the center of each one. Mix all of those samples together, which, collectively, should total about one gallon. Place this mixture of samples in a resealable plastic bag.

Your agent can tell you where to send the hay for testing. Currently, the cost is an average of $15 for the entire test. You will learn not only what the protein percentage is, but also the calcium/phosphorus content. Also, you will find out if this hay is selenium deficient. A number of other characteristics of that lot will also show up on the test.

There are several things that can affect the quality of your lot of alfalfa. The first

cutting is not necessarily the highest in protein. With alfalfa, protein is probably most affected by the timing in getting it put up. Some farmers wait until it is in full bloom. If you look out into a field of alfalfa and view a sea of purple flowers, it's too late as the alfalfa is in full bloom. At this point, the alfalfa plant is at its most mature stage and the next crop is already growing. If a farmer waits until full bloom or a little past that to cut his field, he is actually taking out the first cutting, plus the start of the next. As a consumer who buys from this lot, you could be getting a lower protein hay.

You must also be careful not to get hay that has a high moisture content or you will run into problems with mold—although a little moisture can actually be of benefit. Some of the "purists," if you will—farmers who pride themselves in baling alfalfa—will only bale at night when there is some dew on the hay so that it will retain the leaves. If the air is very dry and a farmer begins baling, and you see a cloud behind that baler, you are looking at a cloud of lost protein.

Ideally, you will find high quality alfalfa by looking for purity of bales. These bales will be fine stemmed and you won't see those purple flowers.

The only way you are truly going to meet your horse's nutritional needs is to know what you are feeding.

scoops of whole oats per day, broken into two feedings: one scoop in the morning and one at night. Our scoops hold 1¼ gallons.

We also use a supplement that is about 30 percent protein. All the horses get a small amount of this, about one cup per feeding. It works to balance out the overall protein intake to about 14 percent. With the babies, it also helps keep the calcium/phosphorous ratio correct, which aids in preventing ephiphysitis (an inflammation of the growth plates). We also feed the babies a small amount of liquid vitamins and, as with all our horses, Select Nu-Image for

their coats. If a baby stays where he should be on this ration, weight and fitness wise, we will leave him on it. If we see that he needs to add weight, we will increase the oats.

Let's say you have a weanling that isn't putting on weight and finish, or getting as nice a coat at the others on the same feed program. This baby would surely be a candidate for some extra help in the way of vitamins, possibly in liquid form, where they could be squirted down his mouth with a needle-less syringe. Talk to your vet to get his or her suggestions on how to best supplement such a baby.

With yearlings on up, we will start at one scoop of oats twice a day. Again, we watch them to see what their bodies are like and to determine how much to add or take away. When a horse first starts on the work program, one scoop is probably enough, but if the horse is not adding the weight we want to see, we will increase the grain. When we increase work times a few weeks before the World, we find that some horses will need more grain to hold their weight. (The 2-year-old stallion I mentioned previously was an exception to this rule.)

We never raise or lower the ration is large amounts, but do it with an adjustment of about ⅓ scoop, added or taken away. If we want the horse to gain, but that ⅓ scoop isn't doing the trick, we might increase a little more after he has adjusted to that first addition of the ration. But we never increase it by a lot all at one time.

Most of our horses eat whole oats, but occasionally we get a picky eater. We add a little sweet feed to the oats to encourage horses like this to eat. Once the horse's appetite is well established, we can usually stop giving him the sweet feed and he will be fine with the oats.

We also have some horses who won't eat their alfalfa if it falls from the rack of the feeder down onto the top of the grain in our combination feeders. A horse like this sometimes does better if his hay is put on the stall floor. But, to add to the woes, this might also bother him because he will walk the stall and mix the alfalfa in with the shavings, then not want to eat it. For a horse like this, we will mount a hay-only feeder on his back wall, away from his grain tub. These feeders are built like hay bags in that the horse has to reach in and pull the hay out.

The trick is to bend to their wishes to get them to eat as well as you can, but to not worry if they don't gobble up every feeding within a matter of minutes. Horses aren't built to do that. They are grazers whose bodies are designed to have small amounts of food moving through all day. We have some horses that will work all day on their breakfast, but they do eventually clean it up. If they don't, we remove the leftover grain and give it to the broodmares that are out in the pasture. However, we won't give it to them if liquid vitamins have been squirted on the grain. This will cause the grain to get rancid if vitamins are left on too long.

Salt is an important part of every horse's diet. We keep salt blocks in the feeders. Some feeds have salt included in them, so the horse's body lets him know how much he needs to work on a salt block.

Most of our horses eat whole oats.

There are many good commercial sweet feeds and supplements on the market today. They are labeled so you can see the protein and nutrient contents. We use oats, but that does not mean it will be the best feed for your horses. This works for our area, based on how the locally grown alfalfa and grains balance out nutritionally.

One way to determine what is best to feed your horse is to contact your county extension agent. Because county extension agents are involved in running tests on feed grown in their area, they are aware of the content and can help you develop a feeding program that supplies the necessary protein and nutrients. Your county extension agent can also supply you with publications from a variety of sources, such as Oklahoma State University, Kansas State University and Texas A&M, where studies on feeds and feeding are being conducted.

I asked the Kansas State University Extension Agent for our county, Dave Kehler, to give you some guidelines in choosing feeds, especially where alfalfa is concerned. The quality and content of alfalfa varies a great deal throughout the United States. In the sidebar, "Testing Hay," Dave tells you how you can have your alfalfa tested for nutrient content.

A Look At Our Exercise Program

Jutting corners on an exercise regimen is like cheating on daily grooming. Sooner or later, it's going to reach up and bite you. Our exercise program is intense, not in the amount of time the horses work, but in the consistency with which we work them. Our horses are worked six days a week.

We work our horses in one of two ways: inside the barn in our pen, or outside, weather permitting, on a 2-acre sloped track. Besides the obvious individual needs of each horse, the weather and time of the year have a real bearing on our program.

In the warmer months when we work horses outside, older horses work an average of 10 to 12 minutes. In this amount of time, it's easy to get their bodies tight and get a sweat going. We want these benefits but not a heat-founder problem, so a 12-minute maximum is our guideline during most of the year. This changes as the goal—the World Show in November—gets closer.

About 45 to 60 days before the World, when the weather is cooler, we bump up the average workout times from 15 to 20 minutes. Not only does it take longer to build a good sweat during this time of year, it also helps us to get them peaked for the big show.

After the World, we have a few weeks to let the horses down a little before we haul to Denver in January for the National Western Stock Show. You can't hold a horse at peak for long, so we go ahead and back them off, down to about 12 minutes of exercise. We also cut back a little on feed.

During the cooler months, we work our horses indoors, starting at about 8 a.m.—later if the pen is really cold. But in the summer, when tem-peratures soar and humidity rises, we will often start working the horses before 6 a.m., both to eliminate problems of heat and to keep the sun off their coats.

Weather affects our exercise program quite a bit. It also affects the energy levels of the horses. We have noticed that when the barometer goes down, the horses get high. Even after they work, they want to play. This usually means a change in the weather is coming. When the barometer goes up, the horses are far more relaxed and might not want to work as hard.

We watch a horse's fitness level closely when determining how much to work him. When we bring in a new horse and don't know anything about the program he has been on, we will start him out slow, the same way we would with a young horse. We'll watch his breathing as he works.

If our other horses are on a work program of 12 to 15 minutes, but a new horse starts laboring to breathe and gets real hot in six or seven minutes, we stop the workout. We bump the horse's workout up a minute or two a week if his breathing gets easier and he tells us he can take it. He will still be worked six days a week, but his times will be shorter. Usually, in a week or 10 days, we will start seeing some changes in his fitness level.

When the horses are working indoors in the round pen, we watch the clock to keep track of how they are reacting to their workout times. When they are working outside, we figure how many minutes it takes to get around the track. With the babies that are working for six minutes total, it is generally three times around.

If the weather is good, we love to work the horses outside with a John Deere Gator all-purpose farm utility vehicle with a hood (see photos). The horses really look forward to it. This kind of workout relieves boredom, and the horses enjoy looking around at the surrounding pastures, some of which have cattle or other horses. This keeps the horses that are being worked from getting soured by the confinement they experience for the remainder of the day.

If you are thinking about using a farm vehicle in your program, here are some cautions and an explanation of how we break the horses to pony alongside it:

First, it's important to know that a four-wheel vehicle like a Gator is something you must be very careful with. If you allow a horse to shoot out in front of the vehicle, you could hit him and even break one of his legs. If you let a horse get behind it, something could spook him and he could run into the vehicle. If you're not paying attention, an accident can easily happen. We

have never had a mishap, but that is mostly because we are extremely careful in teaching these horses where to position themselves and how to work.

We've had some people watch us and say that they need a utility vehicle in their program. I tell them that if they are not experienced horsemen, they had better wait until they can really "read" a horse.

We don't bring any horse out to work until he is well broke to tie and lead, and has worked satisfactorily in the round pen, particularly if he is a weanling. More than likely, a horse will feel good and want to get ahead of it rather than fall back. We use the same long cotton rope that we use in the round pen, with a chain for control. We are careful not to rip on the horses, and use finesse in handling the rope, telling the horse where it should be.

At first, the horses are curious and want to get next to the four-wheeler. That's why, for at least the first two weeks, we use two people to school the horses. The person sitting on the hood wiggles the chain and rope enough to let the horse know that he needs to move away from the vehicle.

The driver of the vehicle has to stay in tune with the person handling the horse. If a horse should flip out, perhaps just from feeling high,

current facility, we used only the natural cushion of the pasture grass for footing. Gradually, it wore and packed down, becoming too hard. So we started bringing out shavings that had been cleaned from the stalls and spread them over the track for more cushion. After a rain, the top of this footing might appear dry, but we check to be sure it's not slick underneath. Normally, we're not asking the horse to make any sharp turns where he might slide around, but if the footing is slick and a horse starts jumping, he could fall and slide under the vehicle.

Used correctly and safely, there are extensive benefits in using the vehicle in our fitting program. We start on a level stretch, then work an uphill slope—not a big hill, but a noticeable incline. We then work another level stretch, and back down the opposite slope. When the horses are going uphill, we're keeping them at a fast trot, and you can really see them working through the shoulders, loin and back end.

You can't keep a horse laboring like this for a long time, so when we make the gradual turn to a stretch of flat area, we let them level-out on the pace. Then, when we start down the grade, we let them slow and stay at a speed that is comfortable for them and allows them to relax and catch their breath. This works much like the human concept of interval training where the body pushes, then recovers, then pushes again.

When we pick back up to work the incline, it's never hard to get the horses to move out more. Working outside helps them stay fresher and gives them a desire to work harder. We would love to be able to work them outside year-round, but Kansas weather does not allow this.

Depending on where you live, you can work your horses outside when the air temperature is below 60 degrees, covering them with sheets to keep their winter coats from setting. We don't take that chance, however. Usually, when Kansas temperatures drop, the wind rises. We don't want the horses exposed to cold wind.

So even though our inside pen isn't heated like the main portion of the barn, it is still warmer in the winter months than the outside air temperature. Because of the temperature difference between the stall area and the inside work area, the horses often get a surge of energy when they come into the round pen. They may not sweat much under their sweat wraps while they work, but as soon as they are led back into the stall and the warm barn air hits the body, the

the driver has to stop. The handler should slip off the hood, reel out some slack and "go with" the horse until he settles and stops. Then, the handler can lead the horse back up and try again. We try to stay off the horse's head as much as possible.

When the horse is ready, I go solo and take him around myself with the vehicle. If the horse should spook or set back enough that I need to quickly get off the vehicle and go with him, I can just flip the switch to shut it off.

When I'm working some studs, especially aged studs that are likely to bite, I won't go solo. This is a two-person operation, with one person sitting on the hood facing the stud and keeping him away from me while I'm driving.

Regardless of the age or sex of a horse we are working, we are careful to check track conditions before we go out. We want to see good footing in all of them. When we first moved to our

hair stands up a little and the perspiration really starts running under the sweat gear.

When the season for working indoors arrives, the horses undergo a change in condition until their bodies adjust to the new workout routine. Our round pen encompasses a 45-foot area, which is much tighter than the 2-acre track they had been working on in warmer weather. Because they are now working flat and not climbing that slope, they are not using the same set of muscles they used outside. For a while, their fitness levels back off. After about 15 to 30 days, depending on the individual, their fitness levels pick up.

The depth of footing in which the horses are working helps them regain their fitness level. The mixture of sand and shavings in our pen is about 4 to 5 inches deep, a little deeper than the outside track. It provides a good cushion for their legs, but also requires that they work hard enough to get results. If they are lazy and coasting, and just jogging along, we'll wiggle a longe whip at them to make them drive more off the hind end and work at an ideal extended trot.

We don't ask a horse to run if he doesn't want to go on his own. If he wants to run, we'll let him, as long as he is not moving forward with a burst of speed that will likely get him hurt or cause him to over reach and pull a shoe. Being able to take hold of a horse is one of the biggest advantages to using a longe line in the pen.

Other reasons exist to use a longe line. If the horse doesn't work off the line at home, he won't know how to longe when he gets to a show. You have to keep up your exercise program as much as possible, especially at a multi-day event.

If you want a horse that is tight and has all the pop and flair to his muscles that proper conditioning brings, don't short-cut his exercise program. If they are going to win, they have to work!

Shaping Necks

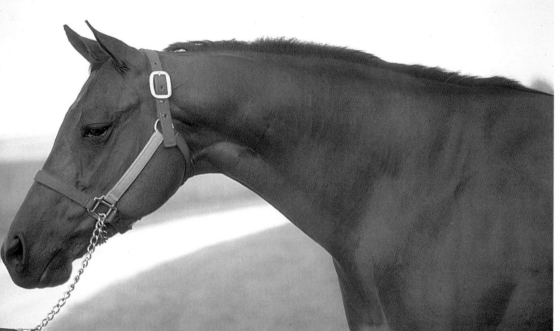

In the chapters on choosing prospects, and manes and tails, we discuss different kinds of necks. In this chapter, we'll tell how you can make a neck look its best.

Your strongest ally in the war against heavy necks is a regular sweating program.

We sweat our horses five days a week during most of the year, moving to six days a week about 60 days before the Youth or open World Show—whichever one we are aiming for with a particular horse.

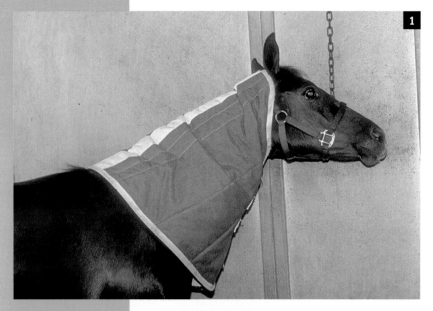

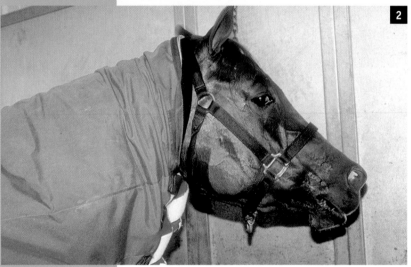

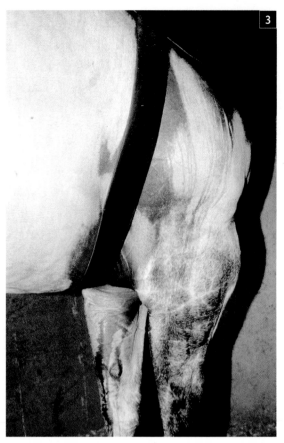

Sweating times vary with each horse. The weanlings only stand and sweat for 30 minutes after they have worked. The average time for older horses is 1 to 1½ hours. With problem necks, we let some sweat for two or three hours, provided the horse will maintain a sweat for that long. If the body starts to cool out, the sweating stops.

We have a note board hanging in the tack room. Each time a horse is brought in from working, we write down the time the sweat wraps are to come off. We work the horses in order, right down the stall row, so there is no confusion as to which time goes with which horse. When the horse's sweat wraps are pulled, we check him off, or erase the time from the board. Then, we watch the clock for the next horse's time. If it's summertime, the horse goes to the wash rack to be hosed down with warm water after the sweats

are pulled. During cooler months, the horse remains tied in his stall while his neck is sponged with warm water, then wiped with a sweat scraper.

It's important to make sure the sweat isn't allowed to dry since this will dull the hair coat and possibly cause discomfort to the horse. It's easy to get the neck clean because we don't use any type of sweating lotion. With the weight and design of the sweat hoods, we don't need it. And since we put the wraps on most of the horses in the barn and then let them stand tied in their stalls while they wait to work, most have already started to sweat before we take them to the round pen or out with the farm vehicle, especially in the summer.

I designed the sweat wraps that we use. The inside material is Neoprene with hook-and-loop fastener tabs that can be pulled tight, from the throatlatch area clear down to where the neck ties in to the chest. The outer part of the wrap is heavy, like a blanket hood with the face section removed. It also has hook-and-loop fasteners that can be pulled tight to discourage air from hitting the neck. You can't stop all the air from getting inside, but the tighter the sweat wrap, the more the horse will sweat.

We use sweats in different sizes, from weanling to full horse. These sweats vary in cut, depending on what the horse needs for his shoulders. Some are for full-shoulder sweating, some for half-shoulder. The reason is that many halter horses today don't have enough shoulder to begin with. We don't want to remove bulk from that area, so on horses like these, we will use the half-shoulder wrap.

How fast and how much a horse sweats has a lot to do with his metabolism. Some horses are easier to get a good sweat on than others. A high-strung, more tightly wound horse will sweat much faster than a "cold-blooded" one. As you work with your horse, you'll notice his sweating tendencies. This will help you decide how long he will need to stand tied in order to sweat.

If your horse is not sweating well, he might have an electrolyte imbalance. If a horse is not visibly sweating, he is heating up on the inside of his body and the heat is not being released through his skin in the form of sweat. Have your vet check your horse and ask what he or she recommends for this problem. We use a powdered electrolyte supplement that we put in the grain.

Generally, horses will sweat white foam when they first start the fitting program. When they become really fit, the sweat will run clear. We've had some exceptions to the rule, but we have noticed that shortly before the World Show, none of our horses will foam.

One point you have to consider when starting a sweating program is how the horse is in his body. For instance, 45 days before an American Paint Horse Association World Show, we were given a yearling stallion to fit. We needed to put some weight on him and worried that regular sweating would prevent us from adding that body bulk. In most cases, upping the feed to add that weight would cause an increase in the weight on the neck, but not on this horse. He had a beautiful neck, slender and tying in high at the chest. Added fat couldn't possibly ruin it. So we only sweated him occasionally and kept adding body bulk.

We had the opposite problem with a Paint mare who was leaving the 3-year-old classes and going into the aged mare division. Weight went right to her neck because of the way she was built. She had never been a big, heavy-set mare when she was younger, so during that time, her neck and heart-girth were her best assets. But when we tried to spread her out and put the

weight on her to make her fit the picture of an aged mare, her neck just ballooned up. If we had kept her weight down to fight the neck problem, she would have continued to look like a 3-year-old with a nice neck, but wouldn't have had the bulk to be competitive in the aged-mare classes.

Some horses who are even younger than this mare are just plain obese, with big, cresty necks. You can see some improvement with sweating a neck on a horse like this, but if you have enough time before the show, put the horse on a diet. You don't want to jeopardize his health or growth, but rather just cut him back until his body lightens up and his neck gets down to where you want it. Then start putting the weight back on him gradually, using a regular sweating program to keep the neck down while the body gets its bulk. While this wouldn't have worked with the mare mentioned above, it certainly will with many horses.

The need to lay up a horse can throw a monkey wrench into a sweating program. For cases like this, we varied a design on our neck sweats so we can insert two heating pads. This works

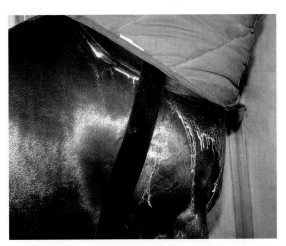

Generally, horses will sweat foam when they first start the fitting program.

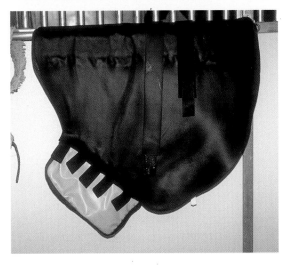

I designed my sweat wraps with Neoprene inside. The outer part of the wrap is heavy material, like that in a blanket hood.

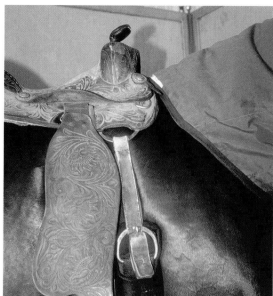

really well with Neoprene lining on the sweat hood. This way, while the horse is recovering from an injury or other problem, he can just be tied up, and the electric hood plugged in. No time is lost in the sweating program. This also works for horses that might be stabled in unheated barns during the cooler months.

Another aspect to consider in your sweating program is whether or not the horse has enough definition to his withers. For horses that don't, we work them from the ground with a lightweight saddle (without a rider) and leave it on while the horse sweats. This method will really bring up a horse's withers. If the saddle has good sheep wool padding, we can use it without a saddle pad underneath. If we decide we want to use a pad, we use a thin one. Using a big, thick pad puts you at risk of sweating down the loins, an area that we don't want to reduce.

To keep the throatlatch area up and tight, we use a sheep wool wrap. This is left on all the time when the horse is in his stall, except when

he is wrapped to sweat or is drying. It is taken off in the morning when the sweat wrap is put on. Following the horse's final grooming of the day, the throatlatch wrap is put back on.

This wrap should be snug but not so tight that it interferes with the horse's breathing or swallowing. We want the horse's head as high as it can be when we buckle the wrap, and want to be able to slip one finger between the wrap and the horse's throatlatch area. If the throatlatch wrap is wrenched on, or put in place when the horse's head is down, the wrap will be much too tight when he lifts his head.

Watch out for scurf under throatlatch wraps. If you see anything suspicious, it may be a fungus. Leave the wrap off for as many days as it takes to clear up the problem and get the hair to start growing back.

Shavings should be picked or combed out of the sweat wrap daily. We also machine-wash throatlatch wraps once a week—sheep wool, leather and all—and let them air dry.

Between the throatlatch wrap and your sweating program, you'll be able to enhance any neck. But, a note of caution: When you are working and sweating horses in hot, humid weather, watch their breathing. If they get too hot, they will pump to breathe, and their nostrils will really flare. You've got to be careful—letting a horse get this hot can lead to heat founder.

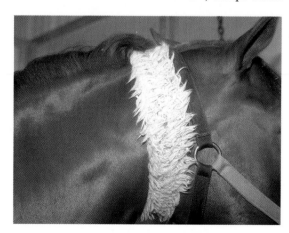

Hair Coats

7

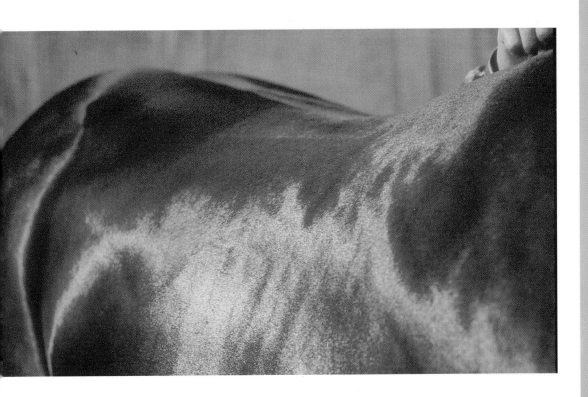

A slick and shiny coat is essential to a winning halter horse. It is also a reflection of his health. Through a vigorous grooming program and analysis of your horse's coat, you can build a beautiful shine.

The biggest component in producing a great hair coat is daily rubbing, which removes dead hair and brings the body's natural oils to the surface. We use small rubber curry combs (mats) that fit our hands well and have some bend and give. They work well on the entire body, but are especially handy to use in areas like the forearms, gaskins and hips.

After a horse has sweated for the prescribed time, we pull off the sweat hood. In the summer, we take some horses to the wash rack right after the sweat hood is removed. We hose them off with warm water, being sure to wash away any foam or residue on the body, neck and legs, and then sponge the face and behind the ears. We then scrape each horse with a sweat scraper, take him back to his stall, and hold him while he drinks from the automatic waterer before tying him to the wall to dry.

As soon as the horse's neck and body are dry, we turn him loose until it's his turn to be groomed again. If he wants to get down and take a nap, that's fine; we clean him up later.

If we don't take a horse to the wash rack—whether it's during the warmer days of summer or during the cooler months of fall, winter and spring—the horse remains tied after the sweat wrap is pulled. We sponge the sweat off his neck with a bucket of clean, warm water containing a ½ teaspoon of Keri Oil. After we have cleaned off the neck, we scrape it. The horse is then left tied until he is dry, then turned loose until the second grooming.

The horses are vacuumed both before they're worked and after they have worked, sweated and dried.

Each morning before a horse is worked in his sweat hood, he is vacuumed and brushed off, so shavings dust and grime doesn't work its way into his coat. As soon as he's brought back into his stall after working—while still wearing the sweat hood—his body is very warm. This warmth encourages hair to break loose, so you will remove the majority of loose hair when you groom the horse after a workout.

We get right to the grooming as soon as the horse is brought in. He is tied up, and we start by using the mat. We spend at least 15 minutes rubbing his belly, back, loin, hip, gaskin and forearm areas. The only time this backfires is in the summer, if it's really hot and humid. The mat will just slide over a sweaty body and offer no real pull. Then, we have to work extremely hard on the second rubbing later on when the horse is dry.

Each horse is tied for the final grooming. We brush off any shavings that might be on his coat, then start rubbing with the mat. We rub for at least 15 minutes—longer if the World Show is close. We don't just rub the body and neck, but also get under the belly, rub the jaw and throatlatch, go down the front and back legs inside and out, and the face. Even if you clip the white hair on facial markings before a show, it still has a tendency to look thicker than the darker hair surrounding it if you haven't worked on the white area to remove loose hair.

After this rubbing, we vacuum the horse completely. We then follow up with a soft brush all over the body, including the face, neck and legs.

If you try taking shortcuts with this grooming, you will regret it. The lack of work will show because your horse won't get that outstanding coat.

Troubleshooting

If it turns out you are working hard on your horse's coat and it's not responding, analyze the problem.

A horse's color has a lot to do with how much shine you can put on him. It's harder to get high gloss finishes on a roan, a sorrel with a lot of roan hairs, some shades of dun, and the lighter

We use a vacuum that is easily moved from one stall to the next. Here, Mamma Cat is guarding it.

palominos. You can get the coat short and slick, but these colors often lack that high shine. When you show, you may have to enhance the shine with a coat spray.

Some horses shed too much, leaving bald spots or areas where the hair is so thin and sparse that you can see the scalp underneath. These horses have a very flaky appearance to the skin and coat and the hair mats close to the skin. This may indicate that the horse has an electrolyte imbalance. Your vet can confirm the diagnosis and will recommend a supplement, possibly one like the powdered feed supplement that we use.

Meanwhile, when you rub this horse, use a rubber curry comb that is worn down and has duller points. The horse's hair will come out too easily if you use a grooming tool with more pull. Also, don't apply too much pressure. You will run the risk of increasing bald areas.

Your deworming program will have a major impact on the appearance of your horse's coat. As you read in a previous chapter, we worm the older horses every 60 days, and sometimes more often with weanlings. If we have a horse whose hair is dull and too long, and he's not shedding like he should, we worm him once, then again in 30 days. We might run a fecal test to make sure he's clean.

Another reason your horse's hair might refuse to shed is a low red blood cell count. If the red count is down, his coat can't reach its potential. Have your vet draw blood on the horse and advise you how to correct the problem..

Medications can affect the quality of a horse's hair coat. The coat can become dull if drugs are in a horse's system. This can be a particular problem with weanlings who sometimes need drugs to fight respiratory infections. In a case like this, you are between a rock and a hard place. You just have to use the medication and put up with the dead-looking hair until the horse gets over being sick.

Whether a weanling is getting medication or not, the hair coats of our young horses are often a problem in themselves. Some of the older weanlings shed out early in the year, and if you don't get them inside and under lights, they will grow back the hair.

Lighting for Good Coats

Our light program consists of fluorescent shop lights left on for 16 hours a day. The eight hours

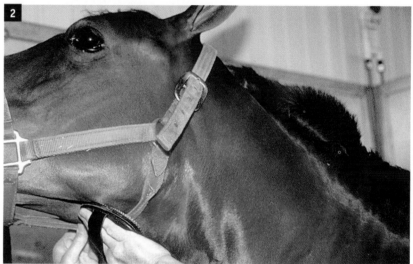

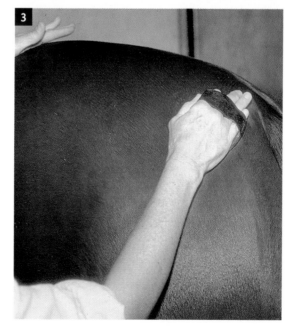

1 A vacuum removes shavings and grime not just from the horse's body, but also from the neck.

2 **3** When the sheep wool neck wraps are taken off, we use the rubber curry comb under the jaw and over the body to remove any shavings or grime.

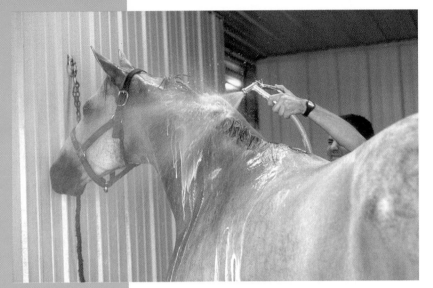

of darkness is just as important as the 16 hours of lighted time. This schedule simulates the long days of summer and stimulates shedding.

Some horses react to the lights sooner than others. Two weanlings we brought in shortly after the World Show in November started shedding within two or three weeks. An older horse brought in at the same time took longer to react to the lights, however. She had been outside and had already "haired up" completely for winter. The babies started shedding several weeks before this mare began slipping her winter hair.

High quality feed and a good supplement that is right for the region where you live (consult with your vet on this) will also help in the quest for a shiny hair coat. We feed the best alfalfa we can buy, and team it up with grain, supplements and Select Nu-Image, a product made specifically for hair coats.

Keeping a horse warm, especially in the colder months, also helps the hair coat. Our barn is heated in the winter at a constant 68 degrees Fahrenheit. We keep a clean nylon sheet on each horse during these months since nylon slides over the coat easily and is non-abrasive to the hair.

The goal is to be able to put a hand under the sheet and feel the horse's body temperature with the palm. If he feels warm but not sweaty, he's just right. In this situation, the hair lays down.

When we work the horses in our inside round pen during the winter, the air is often pretty brisk. The round pen area is not heated like the show barn. Before we work each horse, we put a sweat hood on him and then cover his body with a sheet that is a size or two bigger than the one

he normally wears. We are careful to put the sheet on so the withers and shoulder area of the sheet go over the edge of the sweat hood. If the sheet is underneath, it will rub the horse.

We also adjust the leg straps loosely so they won't rub as the horse's legs move forward and back. If the sheet stays put, we don't use the leg straps at all, but instead will loop and buckle them on the outside of the horse's back legs. As soon as we take the horse back into the heated barn to stand tied and sweat, we pull off the sheet so he doesn't get too hot. By covering him during his work in the cold pen, we have prevented the temperature from setting the hair or causing it to grow more.

If you don't have a heated barn, Chapter 2 on housing will tell you how to adjust blanket warmth to compensate for temperature changes. Always check to see how warm a horse is under his sheet or blankets. You can do this by putting your hand underneath and feeling the horse's body with your palm.

It's also important that you wash your blankets and sheets at least once a week. Otherwise, the dirt in the blanket ends up getting worked into the hair coat.

What if you are close to a futurity or a big show and you haven't had a horse long enough to get him to shed out? If you resort to body clipping, do it 30 days before the show or futurity. After you clip, warm up some baby oil and rub it all over the horse with the palms of your hands as a treatment for the coat. Keep the horse covered up and warm so the hair will look as flat, slick and natural as possible by show time.

Always be on the lookout for "pilot error" that can cause any coat, clipped or not, to set and not shed. Rinsing and bathing your horse with cold water is sure to set his hair. Even with our heated barn and warm water, we don't bathe our horses in the winter.

Avoid subjecting a warm horse to a cold draft, or turning on a fan near a sweaty horse, even in the summer. Drafts are one reason we don't turn on the box fans that are mounted on the grills of each stall door until the horses have cooled, dried off, and had their final grooming.

Just remember how important your six-day-a-week grooming program is to the overall appearance of your halter horse. Your hard work and consistency will pay off.

Manes and Tails

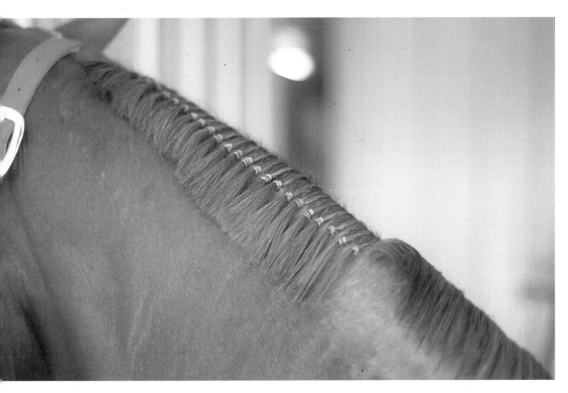

Take care of that mane! Its appearance has a profound affect on the way your horse's neck and shoulder will profile to a judge. A well-trimmed mane with a superior banding job can camouflage conformation flaws or accentuate perfection.

Part of your daily routine should be paying close attention to the mane. Keeping it clean is important. Remember that when the neck sweats, it saturates the mane. In the summer, we rinse manes daily after sweating, and shampoo them twice a week. We put about ½ teaspoon of Keri Oil to a gallon of warm water for the rinse. We are always sure to use fresh water and oil for each horse.

Step-By-step Mane Banding

Whether you band when a mane is wet or dry is a matter of personal preference. If you are trying to keep the mane damp, a spray bottle full of water is a real help.

Start at the bridle path and work back, using a single rubber band for each section, making six wraps.

A comb can hold unbanded hair out of your way as you band the section in front of it.

The comb is also your tool to split the mane into sections.

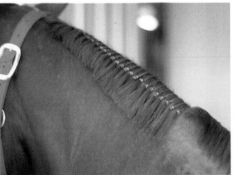

When you reach the crest of the neck, watch the line of the bands so they remain straight and don't follow the contour of the neck if it is cresty or ewed.

Band the top (middle) of the wither and point of the shoulder. Stopping too soon will make a shoulder appear straight.

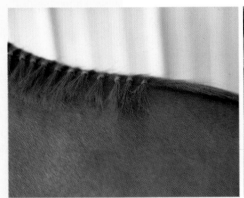

The leftover (unbanded) tuft of hair at the wither should be combed back.

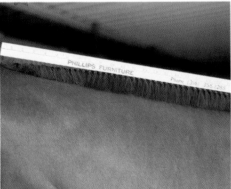

When the mane is finished, bands should be straight enough to line up with a yardstick.

A properly banded mane will look great from any angle.

You can find Keri Oil at many drug stores. It's light, unlike baby oil, which is not only heavier but will cause an irritating build-up if too much is used. And, because some horses secrete more natural oils, you can cause a double build-up problem that could result in scurf. This, in turn, can create an itching sensation that will cause the horse to rub out some mane hairs. Rubbed out manes take a long time to grow back.

What can you do if scurf does show up? We use an iodized-based human shampoo to remedy this. After the shampoo is rinsed out, we rub a lanolin-based product such as Mane 'n Tail into the base of the mane. Because this product is lanolin based, it doesn't attract dirt to the mane.

When we can't bathe horses and they are rubbing from scurf-induced irritation, we use rubbing alcohol, provided the horse doesn't have sores at the base of the mane. Rubbing alcohol is wonderful for manes and for the docks of tails. We pour about ½ cup down to the hairline and work it in with a comb and our fingers. This will loosen built-up scurf. As long as no sores are present, it won't burn the skin.

Since we have a heated barn, we don't use hoods. But if you do, it's important that you wash the hoods often to keep them clean. Be sure they are lined with nylon too so they are non-abrasive to the mane. Your horse can lose a great deal of hair if you cover a dirty mane with an abrasive hood.

Wash hoods and manes at least once a week. If the barn is cold and you can't wash that often, try using the rubbing alcohol method.

After we rinse manes, we comb through them while they are still wet, which encourages them to lay over. Our personal preference is to train manes to the left side. Since handlers usually stand on the left side of a horse, they can easily reach up to smooth it.

If a young horse's mane isn't lying down yet, we try to train it to the left side by loosely braiding it. Braiding is more comfortable than banding and it doesn't scare a baby when you do it. And because you have more hair per section of a braid in comparison to a band, the weight of the hair will help it lay over better. One braid is the width of two or three bands.

When we braid a young horse, his mane is usually 3 to 5 inches long. We don't shorten it until it has been trained. At this age, most horses don't have a thick mane. With older horses, some thinning might be necessary.

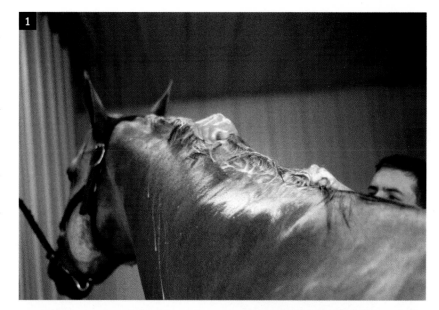

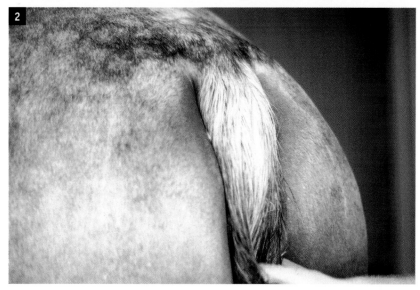

Back in the days before manes were banded, heavy pulling of a mane to thin it was the norm. But today, if a mane is a little thicker, it will lay down easier when it's banded.

We pull the areas that are obviously thicker than the rest of the mane, because at these excessively heavy points, the mane will not lay down completely against the neck unless that hair is thinned.

If we do pull a portion of the mane, we do it sparingly, taking out just one or two strands at a time. If you pull in clumps, you create bald spots. By pulling lightly and feathering an upper cut with barber scissors, you can thin a mane.

Once you have decided a mane needs thinning, your next decision will be its length. In our case, we determine this not only by the length of the neck, but also by how high or low

1 In the summer, we shampoo manes twice a week and rinse them daily after sweating. We put about ½ teaspoon of Keri Oil to a gallon of warm water for the rinse.

2 Gone are the days of pulling hairs alongside the top of a tail.

Pulling Manes

If some parts of a mane are excessively thick, it might benefit from some thinning so it will lay down easier when it is banded. The entire mane probably won't need to be pulled, but rather only the areas that are obviously heavier than the rest of the mane.

It's easiest to pull a mane that is a little dirty, as opposed to a squeaky clean mane that slips through your fingers.

When you pull, take out just a few hairs at a time. If you pull too much in one area, you'll create bald spots. Follow these steps to create a perfectly pulled mane.

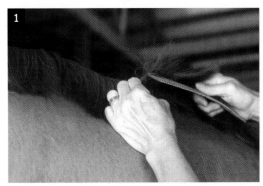

Using a comb, separate a small section.

Select the hairs you want to pull and wrap them around the comb.

With an upward motion, back-comb the hair that will not be pulled.

Pull straight down.

the neck ties into the chest. We also take into consideration the width of the hairline at the base of the mane.

If you have a horse with a long, pretty, slender neck that ties up real high from the chest, the shortness of the mane will not only accentuate this, but will make it look even longer.

With a horse that has some length to his neck but ties in deep at his chest, the mane can't be too short or it will it draw attention to the depth. If the horse's mane is a little longer, it visually reduces some of the depth.

How about the short-necked horse? Keep his mane shorter to make the neck look longer.

To judge the top width of the neck, check the hairline where you have clipped for the bridle path. Is it quite wide compared to another horse? Many stallions have wide hairlines. If

this is the case with your horse, leave the mane a little longer, because when you band it, it will pull down closer to the neck and won't stick out or go sideways. If a horse has a thinner hairline, the mane can be short and will still lay over quite nicely.

We often wait until a mane is banded to shorten it. But let's get into the banding process before we talk about what you'll be doing with the barber scissors.

We like to pre-band the night before we show a horse. This works well when trying to train a wild mane to lie flat. In the morning, we either go back and pull each section tighter or completely re-band it, depending on how disturbed it became during the night.

We like to shampoo and condition manes before we band them. Whether you band a wet or

Shaping Manes with Scissors

Shaping and adjusting a mane, which is done after banding, is accomplished by using very sharp barber scissors. Keep in mind that the scissors are not used to thin a mane, but rather to shorten and shape it.

The most commonly used method for shaping is an uppercut. Holding the scissors at a 45-degree angle, trim only one or two hairs at a time. This creates a natural look and texture. When the mane is then combed below the bands, the hair holds together. There are no flyaway hairs or gaps. This gray horse's thin mane doesn't require a lot of uppercutting.

This sorrel mare has a heavy mane that requires a lot of uppercutting to create a natural look at the bottom of the mane.

A parallel cut (also called a blunt cut) was also used on this gray horse's mane, which is very thin and fine. Only a few hairs at a time are shortened. Cutting this way gives more bulk to the end of his mane, creating a nicer appearance. Notice how the scissors are held in a level position.

With the heavy mane of the sorrel mare, the parallel cut is basically used to trim the underneath hairs only. The scissors are held at a slight angle so that the edge in the front is lower then the edge in the back. The underneath hairs become slightly shorter, which eliminates thickness and helps the mane to hug the neck.

dry mane is a personal preference. A thicker mane, however, bands better when it is wet.

Texture plays a part in banding. A mane that has some body or curl lies easier against the neck. Very straight, wiry manes are difficult to work with. We have used small-rod curling irons on this type of mane to curl it under.

When choosing the color of rubber bands to use, you may find that your horse is in between the available band colors. For example, a dark chestnut horse will be stuck between the sorrel-colored rubber bands and the black ones. In these situations, we always go with the rubber band that is darker than the actual hair color because a lighter band will emphasize an imperfect neckline. It's a lot like when a person with a figure imperfection has to select the most flattering color to wear. White clothing

De-Emphasizing Imperfections

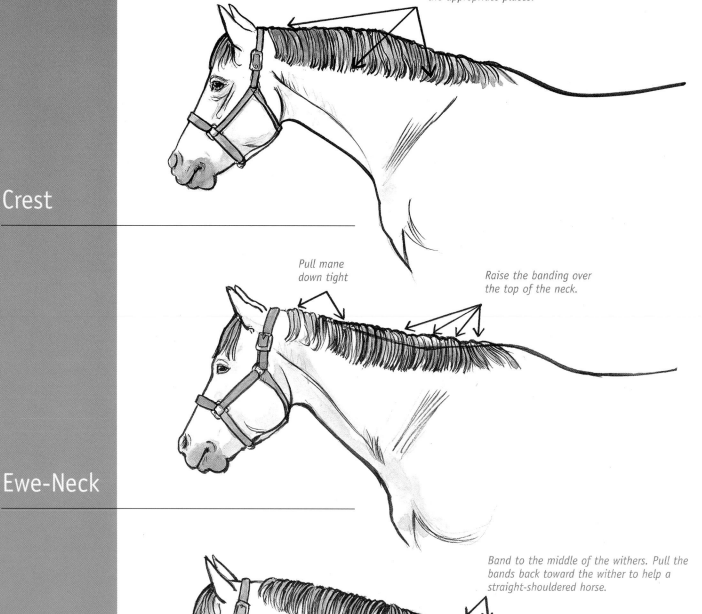

Crest

Make the band level and trim the mane from short to long to short in the appropriate places.

Ewe-Neck

Pull mane down tight

Raise the banding over the top of the neck.

Shoulder

Band to the middle of the withers. Pull the bands back toward the wither to help a straight-shouldered horse.

1 We like long, natural tails that fall just to the upper part of the pastern. If they're too long, we shorten them by using very sharp barber scissors with an upper-cut motion. We like the natural look it creates.

2 A tail can also be shortened in a blunt-cut style, cutting parallel to the ground so the bottom hairs of the tail are all the same length, like a "bob" haircut on a person. The style of shortening is a matter of personal preference, but can also be influenced by current styles on the show circuit. Whatever style you choose, it's best to shorten the tail while it is dry. Wet hair stretches—dry hair shrinks. If you cut the hair when it's wet, it might be way too short after it dries.

enlarges, as the eye is drawn right to the problem. Dark minimizes.

We use a single rubber band for each section of mane and make six wraps. We use the shape of the neck and width of the hairline to determine how wide to make the bands. If a hairline is thick, we can band a little wider with more hair in each section. These bands will pull tighter and lie flatter to the neck. If you band with small sections on a thick hairline, the sections tend to pop up. With any band section, it helps to pull a single, middle, underneath hair—one from the base of the hairline—straight down to act as an anchor.

It's amazing how you can improve a horse's profile with a good banding job. By pulling the tension accordingly, you can fill in the dips on a ewe-necked horse, or minimize a crest. If a horse is straight-shouldered, you can camouflage that area. If a horse has a nice slope to his shoulder, you can call attention right to that asset.

When you show your horse, try to get a spot in line with where the horse is profiled by the judge on the mane side.

On a ewe-necked horse, a section of the neck dips (see diagram on page 54). On the straighter part of the neck, you need to band tightly, with the sections pulled down and snug against the neck. In the shallow area, where the neck ewes, band looser so it adds some height to the dip. The entire top of the neck will look more even. Then, using your scissors, trim the bottom of the mane

so it is perfectly even and not longer where the bands are snug, or shorter where they are looser.

With a cresty neck, trim the bottom of the mane so that it doesn't follow the rise and fall of the neck, and moves straight from the front to the back. When you band, pull tightest at the very peak of the crest. At the front and back of the crest, the tension should be equally tight. This will fill in and blend the areas.

Watch the line of the rubber bands. They should be straight enough to fall in a line with a yardstick, and not follow the contour of the neck. The rubber bands as well as the bottom of the mane, should be straight so the horse's neck will look best on the mane side. On the off-mane side, however, the neck will still appear cresty. That's why I suggest you get in a line where the judge will stand on the mane side to profile your horse when you show.

How far back should your bands extend? We like to band to the top, or middle, of the wither and point of the shoulder. Stopping in front of the shoulder makes a shoulder appear straight. Rather than pulling those bands and the leftover tuft of wither hair straight down, we like to pull the bands back. This makes a horse's shoulder appear nicely sloped and creates a prettier look where the withers tie into the back.

Once the mane is banded, we adjust the length as necessary, using very sharp barber scissors. Most of this is done with a 45-degree angle upper-cut, clipping no more than three or

"Socking" the Tail

If flies are a problem in your barn, your horse can lose a lot of tail hairs by consistently swishing at these pests. Commercial tail bags are available at tack shops and though catalogs. If you don't have a bag, you can cover the tail with a cotton tube sock to protect it.

Braid the tail when it is dry. Cover it with the sock and tie it on. It's best not to leave the sock on more than two or three days at a time, without unbraiding and shaking out the tail, then rewrapping it. The braid works against you if it's left on too long, as it can actually cause hair loss. In the case of mares that might urinate on their tails, it's best to rewrap often with a clean tube sock.

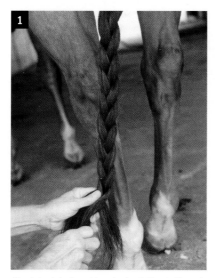

Start just below the dock of the tail and braid it all the way to the end, then secure with a braidette band (the same type used to band manes).

After cutting the top of the tube sock into four strips, about four inches long (for ties), slide it, wrong side out, on your arm, sort of like a sock puppet. Through the sock, use your fingers to grip the bottom of the tail braid.

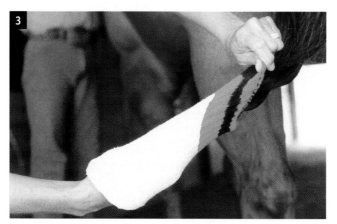

Keep holding the end of the braid as you use your free hand to slide the sock up the tail so it is right side out.

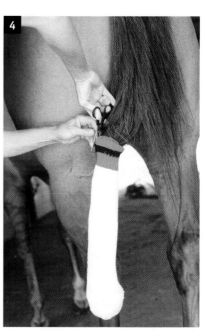

Slide the sock all the way to the top, to where the braid starts just below the end of the dock.

Weave the cut ends of the sock through the braids and tie in flat knots.

four hairs at a time. This creates a very natural look to the mane.

With many horses, you can do the entire process with the upper-cut. But, with a thicker mane, or one that wants to curl under, the mane won't lay flat against the neck unless the underneath hairs are cut a little shorter than the outer surface hairs. If you leave the underneath hairs as long as those on top, the top hairs pull away from the neck. The solution is to use a parallel cut. Hold your scissors parallel to the row of rubber bands and snip just a few underneath hairs at one time. Never use the parallel cut to do the entire mane.

Once this process is complete, and shortly before we are ready to show the horse, we pat the mane with foam mousse to keep it flat. Most of the mousse will evaporate, but if it seems there is too much on the mane, we gently blot the excess with a rag. We then apply a mane tamer to hold everything in place until just before the class.

Luxurious Tails

We like long, natural tails that fall just to the upper part of the pastern. If a tail is too long, we shorten it to the pastern point by taking a hold of the end, twisting it, then gently shredding at an angle with a sharp pocket knife so the end of the tail becomes tapered. Some people cut them off square, but that is not the way we like them.

How long the tail grows is influenced by the length of the horse's dock. The shorter the dock, the shorter the tail. The more dock, the more tail. Some horses have a hook at the end of the dock, and it's hard to grow a long tail with this type of dock.

Gone are the days of pulling hairs alongside the top of the tail. Before a class, we put styling mousse up on that area and just smooth down the hairs. If you are lucky, your horse's tail won't be real thick in that spot.

When we showed World Champion Pure Play, he had a gorgeous tail. It was naturally narrow at the top, then flared and fluffed out as it went down. This is the ideal. But one yearling filly we had in the barn at the same time was real thick-haired in the middle of her dock. A first thought might be to thin the thick part a little. But often when you start something like that, you soon wind up with the entire tail out of proportion. That filly was not real heavy at the base of the tail, so if we had pulled above that

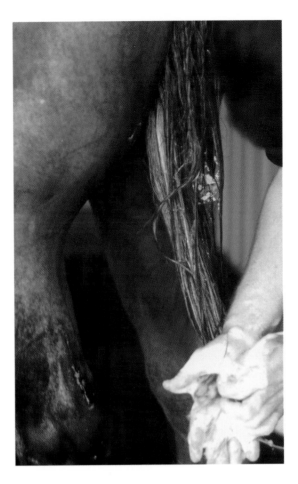

We wash and condition tails before a show, then spray them generously with a product such as Show Sheen.

point, the lower portion would never have achieved its thickness.

We don't like to see any hairs pulled out unnecessarily, so we are very careful with our horses' tails every day. We don't comb them out at home. Instead, we tie longer tails in figure-8 loops (see page 58) after they have been washed, and while they are still wet. This keeps a horse from stepping on a long tail when he is standing in deep shavings.

Because we have an automated fly control system in our barn, our horses aren't constantly swishing their tails at flies—something that can cause a great deal of hair loss. If you don't have an automated fly control system or a way to fog for flies, braid the tail from just below the dock down and put it in a tail bag or a sock so the ends won't break off (see page 56). With mares, it's important to keep the urine out of the tail hairs. If a tail has been bagged, be sure to take the tail down once or twice a week and wash it.

We wash and condition tails before a show and spray them generously with a grooming product like Show Sheen. This allows us to easily comb through the tail and remove tangles without losing any hair. The only time we comb

Tail Figure-Eights

Tying several figure-eights in a tail helps keep it from tangling. If the tail is ground length, the figure-eights will keep it off the ground. Another plus is that the additional weight of the figure-eight stimulates tail growth.

The figure-eights stay in place best if they're formed while the tail is wet. However, if you're at a show, consider working on the tail while it's dry so kinks and curls won't form.

If the figure-eights are made with small amounts of tail hair, they will better stay in place.

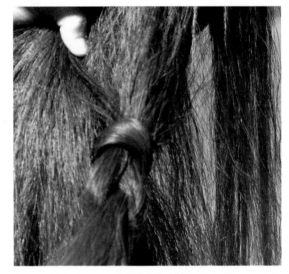

Demonstrated on a dry tail, this is the first of several figure-eights that will be added.

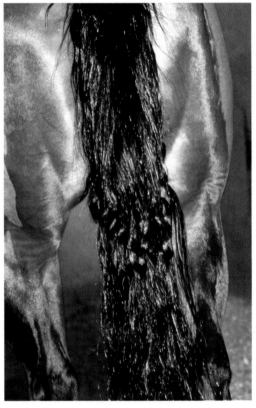

This mare's thick wet tail has had a lot of figure-eights put in it to keep it off the ground

through a tail is after such a product has been applied.

Some horses rub the tops of their tails against their feeders or stall walls. If your horse is doing this, you have to do some detective work to find out why. One possibility is that the tail may be out of joint. A vet who practices chiropractic can pop it back into place.

Or, there may be a problem with your deworming program. When babies rub their tails, a pinworm infestation is often present. A fecal check will tell you for sure if this is the case.

When horses are worked and they sweat, some of this sweat attracts dust. This combination of dust and sweat dries under the tail, around or in the rectum, and near the vulva, nipples or testicles. Some horses will also secrete a substance from the rectum that is so irritating it prompts them to rub their tails.

Part of your daily grooming program should include checking under the tail and cleaning with a rag where necessary.

Mares tend to get dirty in the bag area, between their nipples. If this area isn't cleaned regularly, a mare may rub her tail.

If you find a dry flaky material on the dock of the horse's tail, work some rubbing alcohol or Listerine into it. This will help remove the debris. Follow with a product like Mane 'n Tail, and work it in to condition and moisturize the tail.

Hoof Care, Trimming and Shoeing

I spent eight years as a horse shoer, but with the time demands of fitting and showing halter horses, I no longer have time to shoe. Instead, Richard Clower, a farrier from Winfield, Kansas, trims and shoes my horses.

Richard and I both agree that whether you are dealing with a halter horse, a race horse, a pleasure horse or a rope horse, it all boils down to one basic principal: A horse must be shod like he's made—that is, at the same angle as the pastern and shoulder.

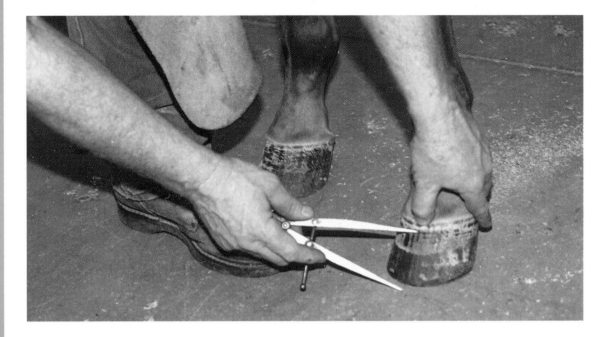

We also agree that you can't correct crooked legs or bad structure, but you can straighten a hoof if it's thrown off a little. And sometimes you can twist a hoof and make it stand straight. But any correction has to be done early before the bone is set so you don't damage the structure of the horse.

I asked Richard Clower to describe his trimming and shoeing methods for halter horses.

Foot Care

By Richard Clower

The most important aspect of trimming is starting young. We trim Denny's colts every four or five weeks from the time they are on their mothers.

One reason to start early is that when babies experiment with grazing, they spread their legs to compensate for the relative shortness of their necks so they can reach the ground. This wears off the insides of the hooves. In order to level them back out, you have to take off more on the outside. To avoid producing a young horse that will badly toe out, you have to jump right on this potential problem. If you wait until the horse is 2 years old to start correcting this, the joint will already be set and angled out.

Some weanlings stand narrow in the hocks until they grow bigger. To combat this, we trim a little more off the outside of the back hoof. This rocks the hock out and is akin to you standing flat on your feet. If you rock your weight a little to the inside, your knees will touch. Rock to the outside and your knees move away from one another.

The point of this is to get a correct look in front, from the front of the foot up the leg. If the horse toes out a little, you need to lower the outside. Doing so will drop the foot in and the knee out a little. When we shoe a horse like this, the inside of the shoe goes past the foot and a ¼-inch extension goes out behind the heel to support the inside. We are rolling the shoe a little on the outside and want to rise on the inside, so we leave that shoe outside for support. This gives the horse something to land on.

Whether I'm trimming or shoeing a halter horse, I want the foot to appear symmetrical. Mother Nature seems to have put a little more flair on the outside than the inside on most horses, but I work to make everything more uniform. This includes length—I like all four feet to be the same. Once I get the first foot the way I like it, I use dividers to check the length on the other three feet. I trim to a parallel notch drawn on the ground.

As far as angles, I can't say we stick with any particular number. We basically just eyeball the shoulder and pastern angles.

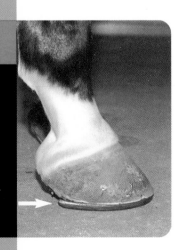

Seven or eight months out of the year, the horses are shod in steel shoes. But in the fall, for the Quarter Horse Congress and the World Show, we raise the horses up 3 degrees with an aluminum wedge shoe on the front feet only. The horses continue to wear regular steel shoes in the back.

For these important shows, we shoe the horses for how they will stand in the dirt of the show pen, not on the concrete alleyway of the barn.

During the rest of the year, Denny is in and out of the show pen quickly because the classes aren't big. The horses don't get tired, so they stand up straight. But if Denny has a horse in a big class at the Congress or World, that horse might have to stand in the show pen for an hour. In this situation, a horse will get tired and rock back on his heel until the dirt touches the bottom of the foot. As a result, the horse won't stand up well. Even a horse with a nice pastern could appear coon-footed [the hoof-pastern axis is broken back at the coronary band] under these circumstances. A long-pasterned horse will look even worse. Shoeing a horse with the aluminum wedge shoe compensates for the rocking back.

Bar shoes also combat this problem. With the bar across the back of the shoe, the horse can't rock back deep onto his heel. We have also had a lot of luck using the wedge shoe. We just don't leave the shoe on all year.

When we bring the horses back down with steel shoes, this helps stretch the tendons and reduces the concussion that accompanies being set up at a higher angle. We also know that when a horse's heel is wedged, no frog pressure results. Going back to regular shoes returns pressure on the frog and sole necessary to avoid the risk of contracted heels—contracted heels is a problem to watch out for in halter horses.

Most halter horses have lived in box stalls almost all of their lives. If they were able to move around at will, it would help their feet spread.

Whichever way we are shoeing Denny's horses, we set the shoe out behind the foot about ¼ inch to support the heel. This also helps with the rocking back problem. I'll "safen" the edge by beveling it—that is, rasping the edge off on the part that protrudes behind the heel—so if a horse should over reach and step on it with his back foot, he is not as likely to pull the front shoe. As long as the horses are under control—such as when they are working on the end of a longe line in the round pen—they are less likely to lose a shoe. But if you are going to turn one loose and let him run, he might pull one off. Horses are more prone to over reaching with the steel shoe than the aluminum wedge shoe because the steel shoe is at a 3-degree lower angle. This way, the horse won't break over with his front foot as quickly. We haven't had much of a problem either way, but we do take those precautions.

When I shoe Denny's horses, nail choices come into play. We shoe the horses so often that we run the risk of winding up with a foot full of big holes where past nails have been.

To combat this, I don't use a back nail since the horses are shod every five weeks or so. I also use a smaller nail on halter horses than I do on other types of horses. With a keg shoe, the general procedure is to use a size 5 nail, but I use a 4½. With a halter horse, you won't have a situation where the smaller nail causes the shoe to slide off, as it might with a reining or cutting horse.

The same goes for both front and back shoes. Lately, I've been using 4½ nails on rim shoes for the back feet of Denny's horses. I originally bought rim shoes for barrel horses, but found I didn't like them for that purpose. On the halter horses, however, these shoes shape and fit well. On the back shoes, I extend them out a little behind the heel but don't safen the edges because they are not going to step on them.

I carry a lot of different types of shoes in my truck, including different sizes to fit older horses as well as younger ones. Denny likes to start shoeing the horses he's going to start showing early in their yearling year. Their feet need protection, especially at the major shows where yearlings are led on abrasive concrete. Some horses paw in their stalls and wear their toes and feet down, leaving no foot to work with. So Denny has me put a light plate on the yearlings he's going to haul to a show.

Regardless of the age of the horse, Denny likes to have him shod two or three days before a show so the hooves look short and fresh. If you follow this practice with your own horses, you may find a horse will become regularly sore in the sole for a few days after he's shod. If Denny knows a horse has this tendency, he will have it shod a week or so before the others and take off less hoof. With new horses that come in, we may not know we are facing this problem until we shoe the horses ourselves for the first time.

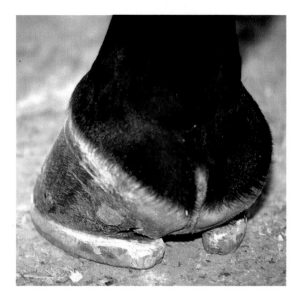

To help prevent soreness, I sometimes put moth ball crystals, turpentine crystals or iodine crystals on the sole and then singe it in by heating up my rasp on the forge and burning the crystals into the sole. This also works with a horse that has corns. This procedure toughens up the sole and makes it hard. I'm not a veterinarian, so I can't tell you exactly why it works, but I have heard that doing this kills the nerve endings and drives them back. I strongly suggest you discuss this method with your veterinarian before trying it.

All in all, we don't have many problems with sore feet. The horses in Denny's barn have good, healthy hooves that grow well because of the good feed and exercise program. And because the horses are in a heated barn, they continue their normal growth during the winter months when outside horses don't.

To help keep feet in good condition, Denny cleans each hoof daily, keeping shavings and sand from packing, and bruising the sole. We also pay close attention to the needs of each horse, whether we are trimming or shoeing. This includes watching the horse travel to see whether or not he is hitting the ground level. Basically, if you get that foot symmetrical—the same on the inside and the outside—the hair line will be level with the ground. The horse will break over the front of the foot and will travel well.

KEEPING FEET SYMMETRICAL

Keeping the hairline level with the ground will help the horse break over in the front and travel well.

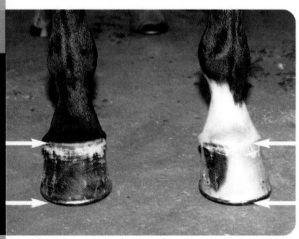

Combatting Muscle Soreness

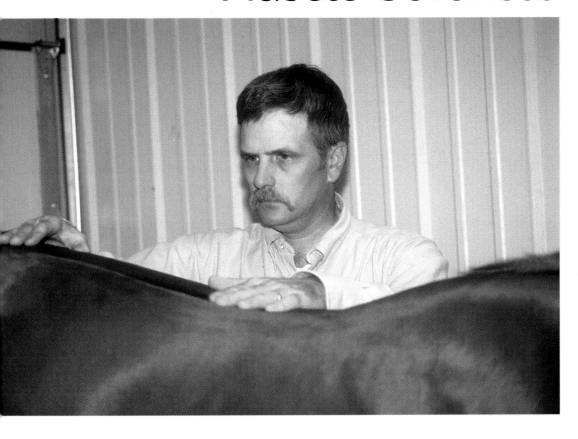

10

We are very careful to prevent leg and muscle soreness in our horses. Cotton polo wraps are placed on all four legs before the horses are brought out to work. This protects them from stepping on themselves. Our horses are worked on well-cushioned surfaces to make it as easy as possible on their legs.

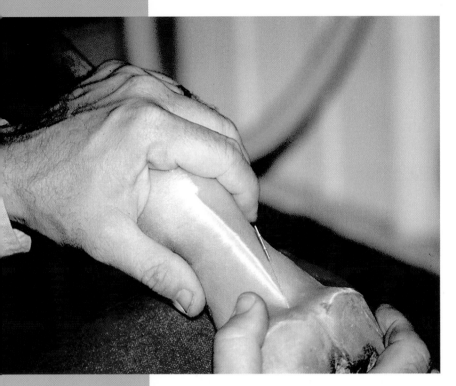

heat, we ice the area. Whenever you have a fresh swell with heat, you have to cool the area before you apply warmth. We take quilts and soak them in ice water, then wrap the area with the quilts and place a bandage over it.

Just as with humans, horses can get sore or out of alignment in almost any area of the legs, neck and body. They can also suffer from growing pains. Several ways exist to treat what ails them, and we use a variety of methods.

Jeff Van Petten, DVM, of Meriden, Kansas, performs chiropractic and acupuncture on our horses. He often uses homeopathic and herbal remedies as well. To illustrate the alternatives in soreness treatment, I asked Dr. Van Petten and another veterinarian, John Brooks DVM, of Andover, Kansas, to explain some reasons for soreness and some treatment options.

An acupuncture needle is inserted just above a weanling's heel.

When a horse is working in the round pen, we don't force him to move out as much as we do when he is outside working on the straightway. Instead, we let him choose his own gait, providing he's not jogging around like a pleasure horse. In those cases, we ask him to increase his trot, but won't make him extend too much and won't ask him to lope or gallop.

We also recognize the fact that a halter horse is like a human athlete. If you take it easy with him when he's first starting out on an exercise program, his muscles will have a chance to build up. Then, as you increase his time, he'll develop muscles to support his joints, and chance of injury will be lessened.

No matter how careful you are, though, a horse will sometimes develop a slight strain or will stock up [have noticeable swelling from the coronary band to the knee and hock]. If I see a horse stocked up but not lame, I still work him. But if he is obviously sore, I hand walk him to see if he moves out of it. If he doesn't, I have the vet check him out as soon as possible.

Sometimes the vet prescribes hand walking until the horse is ready to work on the regular program again. If weather permits, we take the horse outside and walk him in a straight line. If we have to work inside, we hand walk him in both directions in the round pen, being careful not to cut the circle tight, which adds stress to the injury.

If a horse has fill in the tendon and we feel

Alternative Medicine

By Jeff Van Petten, DVM

I was first exposed to equine chiropractic and acupuncture in 1989 when my wife's barrel horse developed neck problems, along with shoulder and stifle injuries. The mare responded immediately to chiropractic and acupuncture and was back competing within two or three days after treatment. I was so impressed with this success that in the fall of that year, I attended an International Veterinary Acupuncture Society (IVAS) course and became certified. That led to training in chiropractic by the American Veterinary Chiropractic Association (AVCA), as well as the study of other alternative medicine remedies, specifically homeopathy and herbs.

Acupuncture and chiropractic can help with a number of problems that halter horses might develop. A horse might be sore in the stifle or shoulder. You may not see visual swelling or a lot of noticeable lameness, but when you watch the horse move, he is just not quite right. The benefit of using acupuncture and chiropractic methods is that we find a lot of problems before they become severe enough to show up as lameness. We manage to avoid this in many cases because we have headed it off at the pass.

As part of some acupuncture treatments, the needle is heated.

When you're trying to convey an image of soundness to the person who judges your halter horse, a chiropractic problem in the horse's body can translate to apparent lameness. You might have a horse that has a problem with his rib cage, causing him to be sore under his shoulder. To the judge, the horse will look sore in the foot.

When a rib is out of adjustment, the problem can manifest itself in other ways. A halter horse I recently worked on was not extending the leg on the side where the rib was out because her shoulder was stiff. She was raising her leg and slapping the foot down. This mare's neck was also out of alignment.

A horse can be sore in the lumbar area and that may translate to a stiff back leg. Or you can have a problem that is making him sore in the back end and manifesting itself in the front.

When I first examine a horse, I palpate at the poll and work down the neck, back and loin. I check the acupuncture points and watch how the horse reacts. I can feel which points are deficient and which are stronger. Through palpation, I also check the vertebral alignment and the rib cage. If I have to adjust a rib using chiropractic techniques, I find acupuncture helps soothe the pain and muscle spasms that accompany the problem.

A number of problems can be helped by acupuncture. Arthritis problems can plague even young horses, and laminitis, soreness in tendons from minor strains to a bow, and bruised feet are not uncommon in halter horses. Fast-growing weanlings and yearlings can suffer from a lot of joint pain associated with growth. Even a young horse devoid of ephiphysitis can still be sore.

In addition to the use of "dry" needles, different types of acupuncture therapies exist. Moxabustion is a process of heating the needles and burning in herbs on or above the skin over the acupuncture points. Another method, aquapuncture, is performed by injecting solutions into the acupuncture points containing substances such as B12, distilled water or local anesthetics. With electroacupuncture, shown in the photographs on page 66, devices are attached to the needles to provide electronic stimulation through the skin to underlying nerve structures.

The needles aren't always inserted directly into the area of the swelling or pain. When dealing with a swollen joint, needles may be placed around the area and in other parts of the body as well. This system of medicine treats the whole horse and attempts to balance it, unlike Western medicine which works on one specific area.

Before you say, "My horse would never stand for that," let me add that less than 5 percent of horses have to be sedated for acupuncture. A small percentage of horses need a lip chain or twitch. The vast majority don't mind the treat-

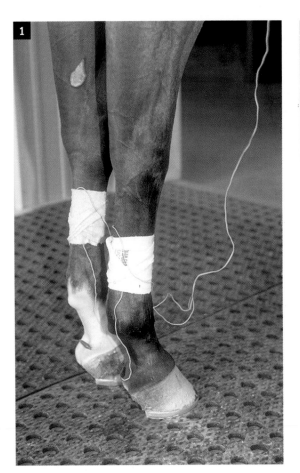
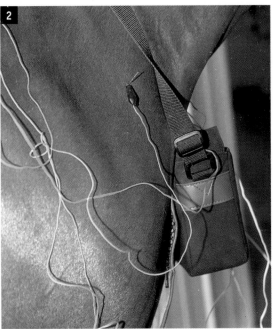

Treating Soreness

by John Brooks, DVM

ment at all. In fact, because endorphins are released after the needles are inserted, many horses relax so much that they look almost asleep during the procedure.

Along with chiropractic and acupuncture therapies, I often use alternative medicines in the form of homeopathic remedies and herbs. You can use homeopathic remedies to treat almost anything you would treat with Western medicine as long as you choose the correct remedy for the problem. That correct remedy isn't always the same for each horse, even though different horses may be showing similar signs.

Some herbal and homeopathic remedies are administered as a feed additive, while others are injected. We use a product for sore joints and arthritis that is injectable, but the majority of these remedies are given orally in the feed or just drenched [administered directly through the mouth].

When you're getting close to a show and can't risk drug therapy, the majority of homeopathic remedies won't show up on a test and can be used as an alternative to drugs. You have to be careful, however, because some herbs will appear in test results.

Halter horses are subject to soreness problems for several reasons. First, they spend a great deal of time standing in their stalls. Plus, they are big, heavily muscled horses with fine legs that easily strain. Other conformation traits also complicate the picture. Many have rather straight shoulders, pasterns and back legs, and this predisposes them to swelling, strains and ephiphysitis problems.

Ephiphysitis is especially noticeable in horses that have one side of the growth plate developing too fast or is very inflamed, while the other side is not growing as much. This causes the limb to be crooked. Both sides may be inflamed, however, causing pain and lameness. Wonderful drugs are available for these problems. They stimulate the enzymes that control cartilage production, causing new cartilage to be produced.

Bogs [round, puffy swellings] in the hock are another problem for some halter horses. If you see a small bog, it may mean a minor inflammation is present, perhaps from a strain. If the bog keeps growing, or if the horse has several bogs, he may be headed for joint damage. I see bogs as precursors to other problems, such as arthritis, bone spavins, or with young horses, osteochondritis dissecans (OCD). Drug therapy is available to help treat such serious problems. Some are injected directly into the joints, while others are intramuscular.

Denny's program of working his horses on an outside track is terrific, and it would be wonderful if everyone had hills or slopes where they could work their horses. Being worked up and down grades in mostly straight lines really tones a horse's muscles. Since the horses become very fit and experience less muscle fatigue, they are less likely to develop tendon and joint problems.

Muscles must be strong to support the joints. It's a fact that most people who develop knee problems do so because they let their quadriceps get lax. If a person tries to play football or ski on undeveloped quadriceps, the muscle becomes fatigued and, in turn, so does the knee joint. The moral is that the more the muscles develop, the less stress the joints are going to take.

Still, there will be some cases of stocking up and minor strains with halter horses. When you pull a horse out of the stall and see that he's off, you have to determine the difference between a minor strain and something more serious. It's important to walk him out and see how stiff he is. If he's cranky and his ears are back, you know he's not okay. If you are tuned in to a horse's attitude, he will tell you when something is wrong. Horses are very expressive.

If you take the horse out of his stall and he's a little sore or stocked up, but by the time you lead him down to the wash rack or grooming area, he loosens up, is walking fine and seems happy, bright and alert, then he's okay. You can work him if that is the next thing on his schedule. But if he's very lame, he probably needs your veterinarian's attention.

Oftentimes, minor problems can be helped with ice packs or hydrotherapy. You may have to resort to this when you are stabled at a show and your horse's legs swell or stock up. Most places have cold water, so you can use hydrotherapy on the legs. I recommend running water on the legs for 15 to 20 minutes. Wait about an hour and do it again for another 15 to 20 minutes. In-between the hydrotherapy, walk the horse to encourage circulation. Ice boots can also be used.

Different types of ice boots can help reduce swelling. Some are just pads that you dip in water and freeze before you apply them to the

legs and then wrap over them. Most horses will only tolerate ice for a few minutes. Keep ice on the swelling for 10 to 15 minutes and walk the horse. You can repeat the ice therapy approximately every hour or so.

Once you get the swelling down, you can wrap the leg with cotton or quilts. You want a lot of padding on the leg. Wrap over it with a track bandage, polo wrap or Vetrap-type bandage. The compression will keep the swelling down, but be careful not to wrap too tight.

If this doesn't work, try a sweat wrap. Use one of the cold treatments first to bring some of the swelling down. Then apply glycerin, available at most drug stores. It won't go into the bloodstream, so won't show up on a drug test. Saturate the leg with the glycerin, then cover it with clear plastic wrap. Over this, apply heavy quilt or cotton padding and the type of bandage mentioned above for wrapping for compression. The more heat you produce, the more sweat you will get.

John Brooks, DVM, applies a wrap.

Special Programs

11

Some horses require special programs when they are being prepared

to show. This might vary, depending on the age and sex of the horse.

But three classes that definitely must be looked at, in terms of spe-

cial needs, are mares who are in foal and will continue their show

careers; weanlings who will be shown in their first year; and stal-

lions, where caution must be exercised in their daily handling.

Mares in Foal

Many halter horse owners breed their good mares during the last year they plan to show them. This was the case with Classical Conclusion, a bay Quarter Horse mare by Mr Conclusion out of Van Valley Te Lady by Te N' Te. Classy's case history can help you make decisions on the breeding and management of your own show mare.

Classy was a 5-year-old the year she was bred to Ima Cool Skip. We wondered all year if, by the World Show in November, she would be too big to show. Our firm decision was to keep her on a regular fitting program, and keep her body tight without jeopardizing the baby.

At Loree Quarter Horses, where she was sent to be bred, she was kept in the show barn and worked. They bred her through a cycle and we brought her home the day after she went out of season. The haul was only two-and-a-half hours, so there was little stress involved.

The day after she came home, we put the sweats on her and worked her in the same routine we use for our other adult horses. We think this was to her advantage simply because any time you have a mare on a routine and keep her on it, her body gets used to it. If you don't break that routine, the body functions at its normal rate.

Gradually through the year, her work was increased like the other horses in the barn, from 10 minutes or so up to 15 minutes a few weeks before the World Show. A mistake some mare

owners make is overworking a mare by trying to tighten her up if she starts to show the pregnancy. We were careful not to do this, and we were going to let Classy's body tell us whether or not she could be shown at the World.

We fed her an even ration with all the supplements and minerals she needed to keep the baby growing, but we never upped her feed during the summer to put the fill and finish on her. Because she was in foal, Mother Nature filled her through the flank area. She appeared to have bulk there, which was necessary to keep her successful in aged mare classes.

Conformation definitely plays a major role in whether or not you can show a mare in foal. Classy is a mare that can carry a little belly. She's built to carry fullness through her barrel and look good. One thing that helped her is that she has stretch in her barrel and is deep in the heart-girth. If she were a shorter-coupled, stouter-looking mare, she would have shown her pregnancy a lot more, but the way she is made, carrying a foal actually makes her look better.

We showed Classy during the year she was in foal. In September, she won both the open and amateur aged mare classes at the Kansas State Fair. By October, she still looked good and her belly hadn't dropped. She stayed filled in the flanks and looked great. In fact, she stayed this way into November when we hauled her to the World Show, where she was Reserve World Champion in both the amateur aged mares class (for owner Don Harder) and in open aged mares.

When Classy came home, she had to be acclimated to what would soon be her life as a mother. She had lived in a stall for five years and had no knowledge of outside fences. She also had a coat as slick as a seal. She had been in a heated barn with deep shavings and an automatic fly control system. All this had to be altered. She would soon be going to a home of stalls with outside runs.

We have several stalls in the back area of our barn, which is unheated. Here we wean the horses off the heat and light programs. We put a sheet on Classy and moved her to one of those stalls at night, but put her out in a safe pipe pen during the day, weather permitting.

While the other "outside horses" rolled, sometimes even in the mud, Classy refused to lie down outside. Her expression and playful actions showed that she was sure enjoying this new life, but in no way was she going to let herself get dirty!

There is a strong probability that your mare will react in the same way. Be patient and give her the chance to let down and learn the ways of a broodmare gradually. Let her grow some hair before you leave her out all the time. Remember: she needs to adjust.

Breaking-In Weanlings

Some of the weanlings we show are born at our facility. To give them a jump start on growth, we creep feed them while they are still on their mothers. We use oats and alfalfa to start, then put them on a supplement that keeps the oats and alfalfa balanced out for the correct calcium/phosphorus ratio. It also keeps the protein intake at 16 percent.

This all works to help the weanlings' bone structure and prevent ephiphysitis. Still, there are some babies that grow so fast, they will be prone to problems. They are better off being held back, as far as bringing them in to fit, until their yearling year.

If all systems are go, we start readying them for the show pen before they are weaned, by keeping them up in the barn with their mothers. This way, the sun doesn't burn their coats during the heat of the day. We put them out for a couple of hours early in the morning before the

sun gets bright, or for about the same time during the evening.

We also get a jump start on training. Babies are pretty easy to teach to lead while they are still with their mothers. When we take them out of the barn, and bring them back in, we lead them right beside the mare. We hold onto them so they can't get away, but we don't have to pull on them much. They want to stay near their mothers, so they don't give us much trouble. Leading becomes second nature to them.

If a baby is healthy and doing well, we wean at four months. If the baby has a cold or isn't quite right, we leave him on the mare longer.

During the time foals are being creep fed, we gauge their appetites. If they are good eaters while they are with the mare, chances are they will keep right on eating after they are weaned.

We start them out with a little alfalfa, given both morning and night, but we don't keep it in front of them all the time. Instead, the emphasis is on the grain ration (the same grain mixture our adult horses receive). My grain scoop is about 1.25 gallons, and I start them out on two scoops a day, divided into two feedings. They also get Select Nu-Image for their coats and a feed additive to balance the calcium/phosphorus. They also get Vi-Sorbin, which has B vitamins and works as an appetite stimulant. At first, we dose them with the Vi-Sorbin with a needleless syringe by squirting the liquid on the tongue. Before long, we can put it right on the feed. It tastes so good, we've had very few babies turn it down.

In the mornings, if a baby hasn't cleaned up his grain ration from the evening before, we remove it from the trough because the vitamins will get rancid if left too long. We take the leftovers out to the pasture and feed it to the broodmares. Then the baby is given fresh feed.

When feeding babies, it's important to understand that their digestive tracts can't hold large amounts of feed at one time. Because the large intestine isn't yet well developed, the food entering the stomach will stay there longer than it will in a mature horse. Because of this, we don't worry if the babies aren't cleaning up all their feed.

As a weanling progresses in our program, if we see he is finally cleaning up all of his feed but not gaining weight, we increase his grain rather than his hay.

Getting babies into the daily routine takes

Depending on the baby, it might be two months or more before we feel he's ready to be tied solid with just the chain. We're in no hurry to abandoned the "chain and rope" method. We give the babies all the time they need.

When we start getting a baby accustomed to actual handling, we rig a second rope for maximum control. The first rope is wrapped with the stall chain and snapped onto the ring under the baby's jaw. The second rope comes off the side ring. We keep this rope on when we're brushing, vacuuming or handling the feet of a baby.

With this set-up, you have control of the baby's head, but he doesn't get scared. If he's only tied to the wall, he's going to swing his body back and forth to try to get away from you. With the second rope, you can arc his head and neck toward you if he tries to get away. He can't run into you with his body. If he pulls back, even if he slips his primary lead rope out of the chain, you still have hold of him with the second rope.

This system allows you to break him to tie and handle at the same time. If he starts flipping out, don't jump out of his way. Stay in there and control where he puts his body.

This method works especially well when you're starting to pick up a baby's feet, which should be cleaned daily as part of the routine. Start with his front feet, keeping him from lunging away from you by handling that second rope. After several days of getting him used to having his front feet picked up, you can start working his back feet. Before long, you'll also be wrapping his legs before he works, and because he knows you have control, he's probably not going to give you much trouble.

Since we vacuum hair coats as part of our daily routine, the baby needs to get used to this. If a baby is afraid of it, we don't turn on the motor until we can easily run the wand over his body without him getting upset.

Babies also have to get used to having the sweat gear put on. With the older horses, we'll go in and tie them up, vacuum them, wrap their legs and put sweats on them, so that most of the horses in the 12 stall barn are standing and building a sweat before we start at the end of the row and take them out, one at a time, to work. After each horse works, he's again tied in his stall, where he continues to sweat for an hour or more afterwards.

We don't want the babies standing there, stressed, for that long. We won't tie, vacuum,

patience, with special attention paid to safety. All this gets them used to being handled.

Because the babies were led alongside their mothers initially, they have learned the concept of giving to a rope and have learned the consequences of pulling back. Still, when we tie them, we are very careful not to hurt them.

We use snap rings that are high at the back of each stall. The older horses are tied with a length of chain that is snapped onto the halter ring, but with the babies, we use a different system—one which, by the way, also works well with older horses who are chronic pullers.

We always use cotton lead ropes because they don't burn the skin of your hand if the horse pulls back. We do snap the chain onto the ring at the back of the stall, but instead of attaching the baby's halter to the chain, we loop the tie chain around his cotton lead rope. This gives him some slack. If he tries to pull back, the rope will give and the baby won't hurt his neck.

If a baby gets to the point where he's stretching his rope out too far, we'll put another wrap of chain around the rope, so it's a little harder to pull. Until we get a baby really well broke to tie, we continue to use this system so the rope does have some slip to it. If a baby rears and gets a leg over the rope, it will slide out of the chain and he won't get hurt.

wrap and apply the sweat gear to the baby until the horse ahead of the baby is taken out for its turn. That way, the baby only has to stand about 15 minutes before he goes out to work. When he comes back in, we'll leave him tied to sweat for only 30 minutes. Then, we pull his sweats, sponge off his neck, stand him another 10 minutes until he's dry, then let him drink and lay down to nap.

Sleep is important to a baby. We don't get him up if he's "down for the count." My father was a great horseman and he always said that when babies are sleeping, they're growing. So we leave them alone while they're resting. Later, when a baby gets up on his own, he's tied up just long enough to be rubbed, vacuumed and have his feet picked up and cleaned. He's then turned loose. The next day, the routine starts again. Babies quickly become accustomed to the routine.

How soon we start the sweating program on a baby depends on how he's adjusting to the barn. We might work him a week or two before we begin. One older weanling filly we brought in after a World Show, to fit for her yearling year, had longer hair from being outside. She was also fretting because she'd been out in a pen where she could see several other horses, and now she could only see the horse across the alleyway. When we first worked her without sweat gear, she'd break into a neck-and-body sweat easily due to the long hair and the stress. Our goal was not to let her get real hot, so as soon as she acclimated to the stall and feed (about two weeks after she came in), we started using the sweat hood.

When we first start working babies, we do it in the indoor round pen. The sand and shavings mix is easy on their legs.

Control is an important factor, so we work the babies in the pen with a long cotton rope. Older horses are worked with a chain under the jaw, but with babies, we don't use the chain this way at first.

For the first 30 days or so, we loop the chain through the halter ring and back down to the longe line. A baby doesn't need to feel the bite of a chain yet. The weight of the cotton rope is enough for now. Then, after about a month, we run the chain under the chin. To lessen the pressure, we have a special way of rigging it up. We feed the chain through the halter ring on the left side, threading it through the center loop under the jaw, then on to the off-side ring.

Rigged this way, the chain won't pull up and put a lot of pressure on the lower jaw, so the baby won't fight it. If a baby should get a little upset, however, don't get mad and become heavy handed. Never jerk on a baby's head. Just take a light hold and instantly release. If you're light with your hands, the baby will break himself to the chain and will accept it. His transition to a chain rigged with a show halter will be an easy one.

The weanlings we bring in earlier in the year are 4 or 5 months old. We only work them for four minutes at first, going two minutes in each direction. They're not at the end of the line at this point, so they aren't working a huge circle. We start by giving them 10 or 12 feet of slack so we can be close enough to keep them going. With the longe line in one hand and the longe whip in the other, we can control their heads with the rope and nudge them on the hind end to keep them moving forward. They are contained at this stage. As they get more used to working, we can gradually send them out to the end of the line to work the full circle of the pen.

After the first two minutes, we stop the baby and make him stand before we ask him to go the other way. This is the first step in teaching him what "whoa" means.

That four minutes of work is plenty for a baby whose been brought in to be fitted early. With the older weanlings who we bring in after the World Show in November, for fitting to show as yearlings, we start out at five minutes and build to six fairly quickly, especially if a baby is in pretty good shape from running and playing in the outside pens before being brought into the barn to start the program. Watching how a baby breathes, sweats and how his body temperature elevates helps us determine if it's all right to bump up his work time.

Once a baby is well broke to the line, and to the exercise program, if weather permits, we take him outside and break him to work on the farm vehicle. Chapter 5 tells you how we do this.

It's important to watch the legs of any baby being worked. If a baby is strong-legged and didn't show any signs of ephiphysitis when he was on his mother, it's probably fine to proceed with the program. But if you see any signs of trouble in his knees, or if he's cocking (or buckling) over on his ankles, stop your work program and consult your veterinarian. Don't keep working him, as this will make him worse.

Right after you work a baby, if you stand him

up and he doesn't knuckle over, he's taking the work well. If he's shaking a little, watch to see how long it takes him to stop after you've taken him into the stall and tied him up. Even older yearlings will shake a little after you work them, but when they're taken to the stall and allowed to relax, they should quit. If any baby or yearling does not quit, consult your veterinarian.

Each day you work with your weanling, he will become more accustomed to the handling and will be more likely to accept the daily activity in the barn. When you have him out to work him, spend some time making him stand while you walk toward his hindquarters and back to the front. "Whoa" is the important word here. It's a word you're sure to repeat often when you start to show your baby.

The first time a baby is at a show, he's naturally going to be scared. But every day you show him, he'll get a little better. Exposure is the best way in the world to season a halter horse.

When you bring a weanling into the show pen, stay very close to his head—don't stand out at the end of the lead shank. He needs the security of having you right there. When he's not being judged, stroke his neck with an open palm to help him relax. Don't ask him to stand at attention during an entire class. Let him relax when the judge is down the line. The more pleasant the experience, the better.

Stallions

Warning: Halter stallions can be hazardous to your health! They're confined, fed and fit, and some are quite aggressive. Success in handling a stallion has a lot to do with how experienced the handler is, and what kind of personality the horse has. If the handler is very green and the horse is rowdy, the handler has no business handling him. But, if you have a lot of horse experience, and especially if you have a real sensible stud that doesn't tend to get aggressive or strong with you, the situation might work out. Regardless, never trust a stud horse. Stay on your toes.

Never walk into a stud's stall unless he's at an angle toward you, so you can easily catch him and quickly slip on his halter. I like to have a stud positioned so that I'm between him and the door, on his left side, approaching at his shoulder. I like to meet a stallion face-to-face. This also holds true when I take the stud back into the stall to turn him loose. I want to be between

the stud and the door, and I want him at an angle.

Watch for signs that a stud horse is setting you up for disaster. We had one aged stallion who wouldn't come to us when we went in after him. He would try to back around and block us from getting out the door. Sometimes, with a horse like this, you just have to wait until he comes to you.

When we did catch this particular horse and he was tied up, he could sense if a person was relaxed or was off-guard and not paying attention. When he was ready to bite you, he would just suck up first and grab.

A good solution for a horse like this is to alter the way he's tied. Our normal tie chain in a stall is long enough that a horse can stand for extended periods of time and be comfortable. His head isn't hung high, yet he can't get it too low. But if we have a stallion who isn't prone to grabbing and biting, we run the end of the chain through the halter, then back up to the ring, so it's half as long. We only leave the horse this short while we're working on him, that is rubbing, vacuuming or cleaning his feet. As soon as we're done, if he's to remain tied after we leave his stall, we switch the chain back to its normal length.

When you are working with a stud horse, be careful not to antagonize him. Keep in mind that some studs are so fine-haired and sensitive that their skin gets sore from being rubbed and vacuumed three or four times a day, six days a week. And some are more sensitive in areas than others. Monitor how much contact or pressure you're exerting. The horse will tell you if you've hit a sensitive area, and you can lighten up. There's no sense in doing something that irritates the horse, then punishing him because he reacts to it.

When we rub a horse like this, we use one of the old, worn down rubber mats (curry combs) that doesn't have very sharp points.

If you have a nice-minded stud horse, but he's just mouthy and playful, sometimes you have to let it go. Just understand that he's just feeling good and not trying to be vicious. If you start slapping at him and playing a hit-and-miss game, you'll make matters worse.

Should a stud actually be so aggressive to the point that you have to correct him, avoid the hit-and-miss spar. Give him a correction, then leave him alone.

Slapping at a stud horse irritates him. If

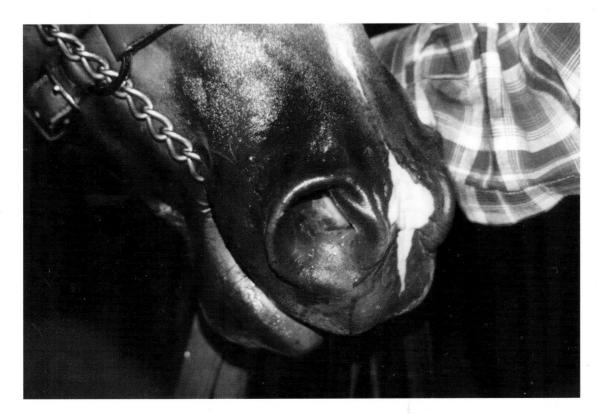

you're going to correct him, do it so he knows he's been disciplined. He has to understand that he's being corrected, and he needs to immediately stop the bad behavior.

Behavior isn't the only problem you might face with a stud. When you're trying to get him peaked, you might run into some special difficulties. If he tends to fret at home, he might walk his stall or weave. This type of horse is harder to keep weight on. Sometimes, if he's fretting, you can tie him up in his stall for a while until he appears to have settled down.

We often have studs arrive at our barn after breeding season, and have to get them in show shape. One 2-year-old came here after breeding more than 30 mares. He was in great shape, as far as being hard-bodied and having a good hair coat, but understandably, he was about 150 pounds under show shape weight. We could have taken him to a weekend show at that point, but not a big one. We gradually added the weight and he easily peaked for the World, where we showed him in the 2-year-old stallion class.

When you show a stud horse, you may need to use a lip chain for control. Even if it's not for control reasons, a chain might just work to help the horse show better.

A few years ago at the World, I showed River City Renegade with a lip chain because he was prone to diddling around. He didn't try to bite,

but he'd put his mouth on me. Whenever he started this behavior, he would lose he alertness. When I used a lip chain with just a little pressure applied to it, he would give me his undivided attention.

That same year, World Champion Pure Play also showed better with a lip chain, even though it wasn't needed for control. Without the chain, he tended to lose his focus and become too relaxed. But with the chain and a little bit of pressure, he would stretch out his nose, stiffen up, and really present himself.

The lip chain tension I use is very light. I apply it just before the judge gets to the horse, and during the time we're being judged. When the judge passes, I loosen the pressure.

A lip chain must be used with finesse. If you jerk on the chain, it can bruise a horse's mouth, since it's run under the lip and over that sensitive area above the top teeth. Used correctly, especially with a stud horse, it's an asset in the show pen.

Basic Training

The most important factor in training a halter horse is establishing

trust. A horse that is schooled and handled through intimidation

will never give you the cooperation and expression that are crucial

to success in the show pen. You get trust and respect by not over-

reacting to or over-correcting your halter horse.

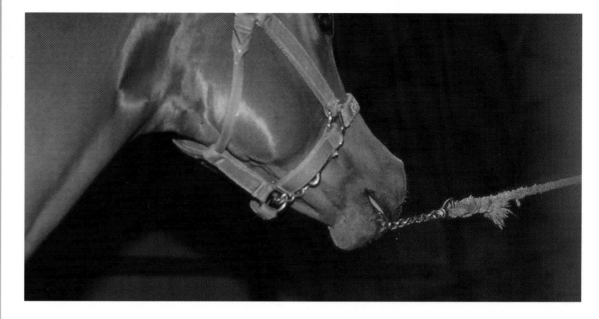

This is not to say that you make a lap dog out of your horse and let him walk all over you. Quite the opposite. But understand that young horses in particular will be scared at first. That's one reason we don't start them off with a chain under the chin; its bite would increase their fear

In the Special Programs chapter, you learned how we handle our weanlings in the beginning: by just looping the longeline chain through the ring and back to the rope so it has no contact with the baby. This is what we use when we first work a young horse in the pen and introduce "whoa," as well as when we start setting up babies.

As the young horse progresses, we run the chain under the jaw, but feed it through the bottom halter ring that is at the center of that jaw strap. The chain has very little bite this way, but does have enough contact to get the baby used to its feel. We don't get rough with the chain; we want to go easy until the young horse is accustomed to it. After the horse accepts the chain, we can take a little hold of him. However, we don't do it to the point of being aggressive.

If a baby makes a mistake and he knows better, I will correct him just to the point that he knows he did something wrong. But I don't over-correct or do anything that will make him afraid of me. If I did this, every time I tried to set that baby up, he would anticipate getting hurt.

The attention span of a young horse is short, so rather than having him set up and hold the

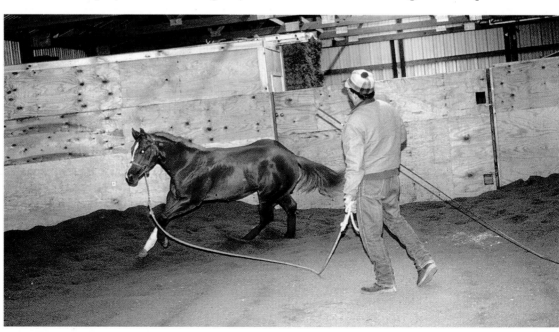

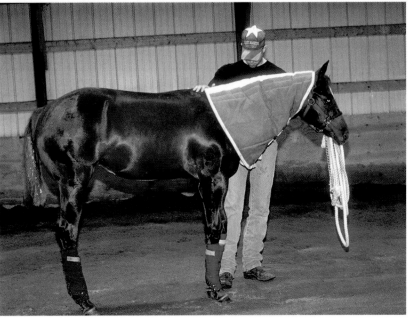

This baby (top left and bottom left) was worked, at first, without sweat gear.

We spend some time before and after the babies work to teach them to set up (below).

position for a long time, we just set him up more often, for short periods of time, in different places. When practicing this with your own horse, just be sure he learns to move only when you want him to.

From the first time I set up any horse, I stand in the same position as I would when I show him—at a ¾ angle with my toes pointed toward the horse's left front foot. And from day one, I teach my horses to look straight ahead.

I don't want to be constantly hassling a horse with the shank, especially a weanling. If a horse starts to gawk and turn his head toward me, I reach up with my index finger and poke it through the side halter ring to reposition the

head. I can even push until the head is beyond the straight-ahead point. As soon as I release the pressure, the horse's head will come back to just the right spot.

If the horse turns his head away from me, I cross over to the right side and poke that side, through the halter ring. When his head is where it should be, I step back to my normal position.

On the days we work the weanlings in the inside round pen, we set them up every day

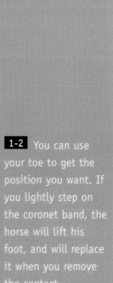

1 From the first time I set up any horse, I stand in the same position I'd use to show him: at an angle with my toes pointed toward the horse's left front foot. I want the horse looking straight ahead.

2 If the horse turns his head to gawk, I will poke my finger through the side halter ring to reposition the head. I can even push until the head is beyond where it should be.

1-2 You can use your toe to get the position you want. If you lightly step on the coronet band, the horse will lift his foot, and will replace it when you remove the contact.

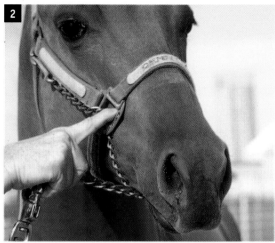

before they start to work. They eventually have to stand still in the show pen when they are fresh and haven't been worked, so they might as well learn now to contain that energy.

If they need a little extra reinforcement, we also set them up when they are done working, before they go back to their stalls. We don't make them stand for very long. Repetition is what gets the point across. We keep telling them "whoa," and we get them to stand while we walk back toward the hip, pull the tail down, and stand off

to the side to look at them. We are careful to keep enough slack in the rope that we don't inadvertently pull them toward us.

With babies, it's important to not pet their faces or mess with their heads in any way that encourages nipping. Hand feeding should also be ruled out.

Let your babies know from the beginning that they can never nip, or even reach out and touch you with their muzzle. It's difficult to show a horse that is so busy with his mouth that you can't get his attention. A horse like this won't give you his respect in the show pen.

Whether we are working with babies or older horses, we follow the same system in teaching them to set up. We used to work off the right hind foot, setting it first, and then working the other feet to it. But we have since learned that our amateur and youth exhibitors could get a better handle on setting up a horse's left hind foot first because it's easier for them to see.

From the beginning, we ask each horse to set

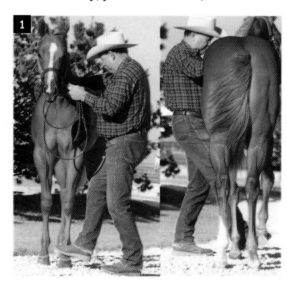

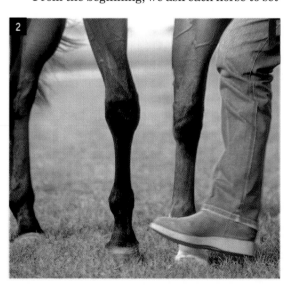

up all four feet, working off the left hind. Even if a horse doesn't accomplish a perfect stance, he will get the idea. When we set him up next time, it will be a little better.

You can try this by leading your horse up until the left hind foot is right where you want it. Stop and settle him for a moment. Then use your lead shank to move him forward or back until the right hind foot is in line with the left. Then start setting the front feet.

To set the front feet, use your toe to move the horse's foot. If you lightly step on the coronet band, the horse will lift his hoof. Manipulate this movement with the lead shank. If you want the horse to move up, tap his coronet as you pull the shank forward. If you want him to move a foot back, touch the coronet with your toe and apply backwards pressure on the shank. As soon as you get what you want, release all pressure.

If your horse is set up and then cocks his back foot, use your toe to get him to stand up on that foot. Do this by tapping the front coronet band on the same side as the back foot he has cocked. The horse will lift that front foot. Since he can't stand with both left, or right, feet off the ground, he will stand back on that hind foot. This is a system that works extremely well in the show pen and saves you from having to walk back to the hip and pull or push to shift the horse's weight.

You might have to resort to hand setting a foot to place it in just the right position, especially in the beginning stages, and often later in the show pen. Do this quietly, then tell the horse "whoa" as soon as you set the foot. Again, if you overreact, each time you reach for that foot or set it down and move back, the horse will expect trouble. He might even move backwards.

Once the horse has become pretty easy to set up, you can start teaching him to prick his ears. Often with a curious baby, you can simply move your hand near his forehead, a little off to the side because of his line of vision. When you know he can see your hand, draw it away and he will watch. Or you can pick up a little arena dirt and hold it out in front of his face, letting it sift out of your hand. Whatever system you choose, he will learn that he is supposed to watch your hand.

With older horses—especially ones you are working on tuning up because they're not as attentive as they should be—you can double your lead shank and tap them on the forehead. This doesn't hurt the horse—he just hears the

We work off the left hind foot. The horse is led forward until that foot is planted in the right place. Next, the right hind foot is placed

sound of the leather and will want to see where it came from. As you draw the shank away, he'll watch it and give you the attention and expression you want. When you get him into the show pen, you won't have to tap him. Instead, just show him that shank and pull it away and he'll watch.

It's important to remember when you are schooling at home, to not ask a horse to hold that look for too long. You can use up the expression by asking for it too much, in the same way you can over-ride a performance horse.

Most horses, at one time or another, are going to fool around and not pay attention while you are trying to set them up. Ripping and jerking on the shank will only get you into trouble because the horse will move backwards to get away from you.

One method I use for correction is to give a straight downward pull on the shank. Then, I immediately release the pressure. If you don't pull too hard, the horse won't move back. Doing this will anchor a horse where he is standing, and most of the time, he will just raise his head, plant his back feet, and perhaps move his front feet a little. But he will be a lot easier to set back up from this position than if he had run backwards 10 feet.

Repetition pays off when you are teaching a halter horse to set up. Every time we bring a horse in the round pen to work, be it a weanling

Extra Encouragement for Weanlings

A butt rope can act as extra encouragement for a baby who doesn't yet lead well from the halter rope alone. As you lead the baby out, if he doesn't want to stay up beside you, coax him up by relaxing the main lead rope and giving light forward tugs, then releases, on the section of the butt rope that has been threaded through his halter. Don't hang on it and get into a pulling contest. He'll feel more of a sensation if the light push of the rope on his hindquarters comes and goes. When he's up where he should be and is moving beside you, return to using the regular lead rope. Never hesitate, however, to tune him up with the butt rope.

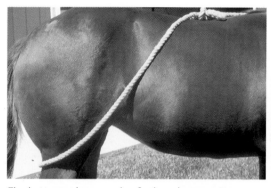

The butt rope loop, made of a long heavy cotton rope, should extend just below the baby's buttocks.

The knot that forms the loop will be on top of his back, closer to his withers than his croup.

Loop the long end of the rope to the left of vertical under-the-jaw portion of the halter, slip it under the horizontal chin strap of the halter near the ring where the regular lead rope is snapped in.

This method allows you to easily handle both ropes.

The complete rig shown on a young horse.

or older horse, we work on setting up before we start the exercise. After working, we might also stand a horse up. During the warm months, When I work the horses outside on the farm vehicle, the horses will be set up near the fence by whomever has brought them out to me. They will stand there while they are waiting for me to make the last lap or two with the horse I am currently working. If you do this six days a week, as we do, you will be amazed at how they soon know exactly what you want from them. After that, you can do it as a daily tune up.

A halter horse must learn to lead straight, with the handler at the head and throatlatch area.

Leading Out

Our horses are taught to lead with someone standing at their head and throatlatch. A horse broke like this will follow your shoulder and always know just where he is supposed to be.

If you get out in front of a horse, and then turn to face him while you try to drag him toward you, you are giving him a signal not to move forward. But if you drop back to his head and throatlatch area, and he moves back, you can too. Just take a step or two backward and hold your looking-forward position while you reach around with your hand and pop him on his hip. Be careful not to pull his head back as you do this. Later, if he tries to go backward, you won't have to touch him. When you step back, it will drive him forward.

Halter horses are usually fresh enough that they want to move forward, but some are so fresh that they want to play and move sideways to get away from you. If this happens when you are schooling, work the horse along a fence. You'll be on his left and the fence will be on his right. By doing this, he will learn to travel straight.

Some horses tend to get playful when they are out in the open, or when they are in the show pen. If you overreact to this situation by running the horse backward, you can get in all kinds of trouble. He will end up flipping out every time he thinks you are going to get after him for a jump or two.

If a horse gets a little rambunctious, take just enough hold of him to stop him. Make him stand a moment, then move him forward again. If he gets real rambunctious and strong, and tries to go around you, stop and back him slowly—only a couple of steps—and then start up again.

Whether teaching a horse to set up or lead out, you can get what you need by not making the problem into a big deal.

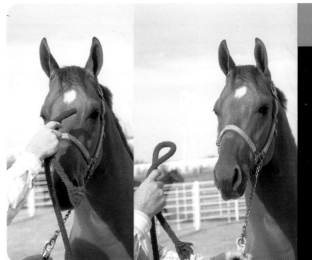

WORKING EARS

To get the attention of older horses, you can sometimes double the lead shank or lead rope and lightly tap the horse on the forehead, then pull the shank or rope away. He'll watch it and give you his ears.

13

Summary of Our Daily Routine

Success comes from sticking to a regular routine. Our routine stays basically the same all year around; just a few differences exist between our cold and hot weather schedules.

Here is how we set up our routine for the 12 horses we work six days a week.

Feet are picked out.

Summer Routine

Our "beat the heat" routine for Monday through Saturday:

❏ At 5 a.m., we feed.

❏ At 6 a.m., we prepare the horses to work. Each horse is tied in his stall and vacuumed. The sheep wool throatlatch wrap is removed and replaced with a Neoprene lined sweat hood. This begins a sweat before we take the horse out to work. All four legs are wrapped with cotton polo wraps, which are laundered every Saturday.

If the weather is cold, we work our horses in the indoor pen.

Sweat hoods are used Monday through Friday during this time of year. Horses are worked, but not sweated, on Saturdays.

❏ Work: If the weather and ground are dry, the horses are worked outside on the 2-acre track with the farm vehicle.

❏ Each stall is thoroughly cleaned while the horse is out to work.

❏ After work: The horse is taken back to his stall and tied to stand and sweat. The polo wraps are pulled off as soon as he is taken into the stall and he is rubbed out with the rubber mat (small rubber curry comb) while his body is still warm.

❏ After sweating: Each horse is taken to the wash rack and hosed down completely with warm water. Twice a week, we use shampoo and conditioners. Excess water is removed with a sweat scraper. The mane is combed over.

❏ The horse is returned to his stall and tied until he is completely dry. If he is almost dry but still has a couple of damp areas and is not hot, he is then turned loose to drink, finish eating and nap.

❏ When we are ready to start the final rubbing, we go down the line and tie up each horse. If a horse is napping, we let him rest and work on another horse until he gets up.

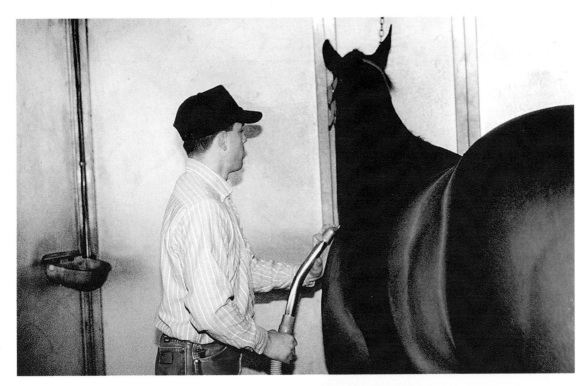

Both before and after they work, our horses are groomed and vacuumed.

When we rub, we do so over the body, legs, neck and face with the rubber mat for about 15 minutes. Next, we vacuum, then go over the entire horse with a soft brush. The mane is combed over. The tail is not combed, as we don't want to pull out any hairs. The sheep wool throatlatch wrap is put on, and stalls are again picked out and leveled. The horse is then turned loose in his stall for the rest of the day.

❑ After the horses have dried and been cleaned up, we turn on the box fans if it's real hot in the barn. (The fans are mounted on the stall doors.) The end and side doors of the barn can also be opened to provide ventilation. Air travels down the alleyway and doesn't hit the horses. The fans are turned off later in the day when the barn naturally cools down.

❑ At 4 p.m., we feed.

Sundays

Horses are given the day off from working and grooming on Sundays. Stalls are thoroughly cleaned and leveled.

Winter and Other Cold Periods

❑ We feed at 6 a.m.

❑ At 8 a.m., we prepare horses to work, using

the same steps as in the summer program. Horses are worked in the enclosed pen, however. If the temperature is extremely cold, we cover each horse with a nylon stable sheet.

❑ About six weeks before the World Show, we increase the working time, both because it's harder to build a sweat in cool weather and because we are working for that ultimate peak. Also at this time, horses going to the World are sweated six days a week, rather than five. We work and sweat Monday through Saturday.

After working, each
horse is tied in his
stall to sweat.

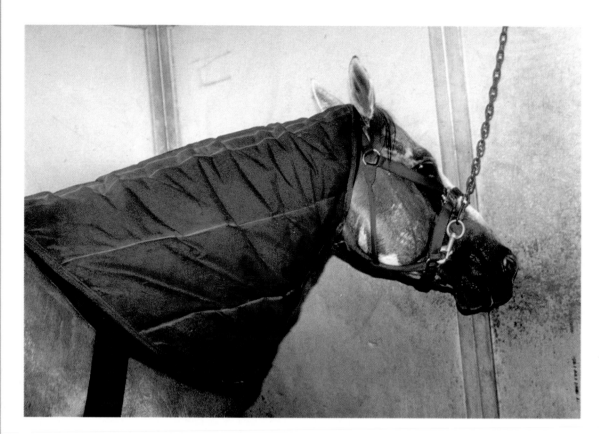

- ❏ Stalls are cleaned while horses are out.

- ❏ After work: Leg wraps are pulled, sheets are taken off and horses are tied to sweat.

- ❏ After sweating: Even though the barn is heated, we don't hose the horses down in the wintertime. After the neck sweat is pulled, we sponge the horse's neck and throatlatch area with a bucket of warm water that contains ½ teaspoon of Keri Oil. Excess rinse water is removed from the horse with a sweat scraper.

- ❏ The horse is tied to dry, using the same routine as during the summertime. (If your barn is below 68 to 70 degrees, I suggest putting a sheet on your horse before turning him loose so the cool air won't cause his hair coat to grow.)

- ❏ The horse is turned loose to eat, drink and nap.

- ❏ Final grooming is the same as in the summer, unless the Congress or World are coming up. In those cases, our rubbing time increases to add that extra shine to the coats.

- ❏ After the clean up, we put a sheet on each horse and buckle on the sheep wool throatlatch wrap. The horses are turned loose in their stalls for the rest of the day.

- ❏ We feed at 4 p.m.

Sunday

- ❏ The horses are given a day off from working and grooming. Stalls are thoroughly cleaned and leveled.

General Routines

- ❏ Clipping: The horses are routinely clipped once a week.

- ❏ Trimming and Shoeing: Farrier work is done on an average of every five weeks.

- ❏ Deworming: We have a veterinarian worm the horses every 8 weeks. If the horses are dewormed in the morning, we don't work them. If deworming is to take place in the afternoon, we work and sweat them in the morning. To avoid getting them hot, we won't sweat them when they work the next day.

Dressing the Halter Horse

14

When we show, we use the same style halter on all our horses. The halter we use is of my own design, with a wide, full inch bar and wide leather. All our halters are designed the same, but come in different sizes since the way a show halter fits is more important than its style. You can make a good-headed horse look bad with an ill-fitting halter.

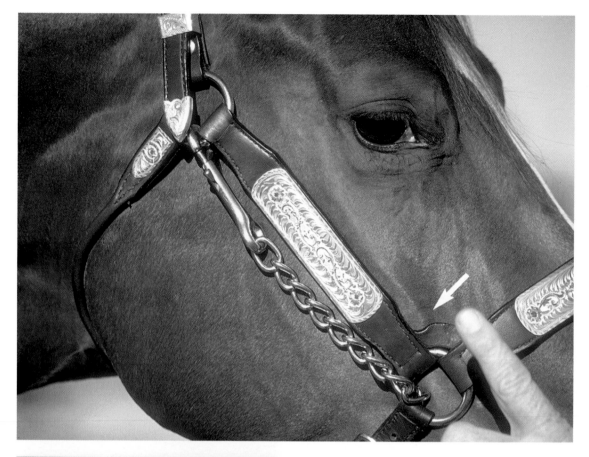

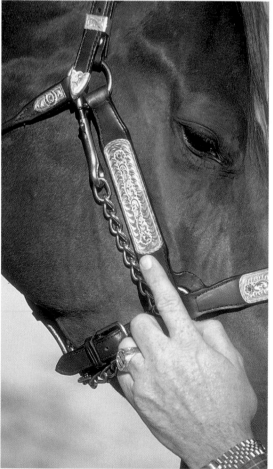

The most important factor in fitting a show halter is to have the side bars parallel up and to the face. The bars shouldn't angle back, which they will do if the throatlatch strap is too tight.

The nose band and chin strap portion of the halter should be pulled up right to the jaw area to what we call the "knowledge bump" on the side of the horse's face.

One style aspect we avoid is the oversized buckle. Oversized buckles hook behind the horse's ears, pinching the horse and making him less likely to put his ears up for you. Our crown pieces are fairly wide, but are beveled to fit right into the buckle so they are comfortable for the horse.

We use halters made of oiled leather. They start out a light reddish color and darken after being repeatedly used and cleaned. Our lead shanks match the halters, and have silver-colored chains to blend with the hardware on the halters. The chains we use with the baby halters are smaller so the snaps will fit through the smaller rings. They also look better on a weanling's head.

All our lead shanks are 9 feet in length. If we get into trouble with a horse, we can reel out some slack until it's safe to take hold of the

In the two photos above, the side bar is adjusted too far back, which creates a bad angle.

This photo shows how a halter should be adjusted.

The crown pieces on our halters are fairly wide and beveled into medium-sized buckles. When properly adjusted, right behind the ears, it is comfortable for the horse. If a buckle is too big, it pinches the horse, and he won't give you his ears.

Waiting at the gate at the Worldwide Paint Congress in Wichita, Kansas, this horse is rigged with the chain we use to show stallions.

horse. This way, there isn't much chance of a horse pulling the leather from our hands.

Show halters are a big investment, so we recommend storing them in flannel-lined halter bags for their protection. You can roll up the lead shank and store it in the bottom portion of the bag, below the halter.

Even though our halters are stored in bags, we normally clean them before we use them. After the leather and silver have been cleaned, we spray the halter with a lacquer made for use on tack.

Clipping

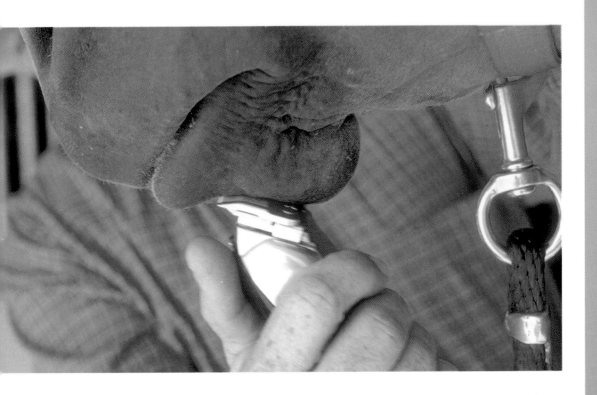

As with other aspects of training, a halter horse has to be taught to tolerate clipping. The more a horse becomes used to being clipped, the better job you'll be able to do. This is especially true with the babies; we make clipping part of their regular routine. It's important to remember that clipping isn't something you put off until the day before a horse's first show. Doing so could result in disaster.

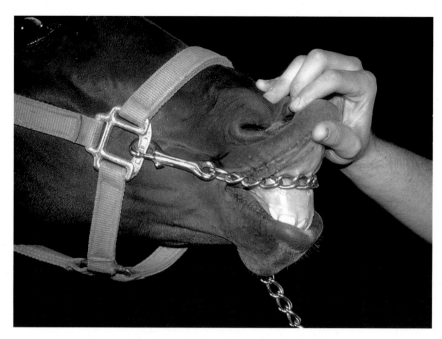

Restraining

Twitching is an option when restraint is needed to clip an uncooperative horse.

If we are clipping an older horse that puts his head up high so we can't get to his ears or bridle path, we will use the twitch after we have worked around the muzzle and nostrils. We either use an axe-handle type twitch with a rope on the end, or an aluminum twitch. You work the latter by squeezing it together, and wrapping the thin rope around the end and snapping it to the halter.

It's also possible to get a horse to stand just by pinching a section of the skin on his shoulder. It doesn't have to be a death grip. We start easy and increase pressure if it's needed.

With a horse that is just a little touchy about having his bridle path clipped, but isn't so bad that he needs a twitch, we gently ear him down. It's not something we do often, and when we use this method, we do it with a great deal of finesse. We are never rough on the ear, nor do we pull it down. We just take hold of the ear and squeeze it just a tad.

A lip chain can also be used to convince a horse to stand still for clipping. This device also calls for finesse. The chain is never jerked. Sometimes, just lightly wiggling it gets the horse's attention.

When We Clip

Let's say we're leaving for a show on a Friday and will show Saturday morning. At home, on the previous Wednesday, we will clip the legs. Leg hair doesn't grow back as fast as the hair on the face and bridle path. And legs are not at a judge's eye level, so they are not looked at with as much scrutiny as the head.

However, this isn't a license to do a sloppy job on the legs. You should do the best job possible, but if you make a mistake on Wednesday, you can back-drag to touch it up later in the week.

We introduce a horse to the clippers by clipping a little at a time over a period of weeks. If we think a horse might be touchy about having his ears clipped, we get him used to other areas first. We clip under his jaw, in the throatlatch area, or maybe his white face marking, if he has one. We don't make a big deal out of it.

If you use brute force on a baby, you are liable to create a problem that will last a lifetime. The horse will come to associate painful combat with clipping. This is why taking your time is so important, particularly with babies. They have a short attention span, so we don't subject them to marathon clipping sessions. A couple of minutes of clipping, done correctly on a regular basis, can work wonders in teaching a baby or any horse that clippers are nothing to fear.

Mainly, we work at trying to get them gentle and accepting of the clippers. A lot of that acceptance stems from regular daily handling, grooming and having their legs brushed and their feet picked up.

Despite this approach, some babies kick at you every time you touch their legs, even with your hands. This can be a real problem once you try to clip their legs. We take a baby like this to the wash rack, where one person holds him while the other sprays water on his legs. At first, he is liable to kick like the dickens, but as soon as he finds out that the water isn't going to hurt him, he settles down. After this, he should be receptive to having his legs touched. When you're ready to clip his legs, he should stand for it. (Remember never to clip a horse's legs when he is wet.)

Keep in mind that we clip a horse before we bathe him. Our horses' legs are kept clean on a daily basis with grooming and, in the summer, hosing down. That helps ensure that the clippers will float through the hair when the time comes to use them.

We clip the horse's head, ears and bridle path the night before we leave for the show, or the morning we are planning to leave.

The location to clip a horse is up to an individual horse owner, depending on how much he or she trusts the horse. In our program, we prefer to clip the horses' heads with the horse standing in its stall. Horses feel more relaxed and grounded there, especially the babies. The stall is the horse's home turf.

Clipping heads in the stall is also a safety precaution. The horse is standing on a shavings-topped surface and if he becomes scared and moves quickly, he won't slip and fall.

To clip the legs, we take the horse to the rubber matted wash rack area, or into the barn alleyway. We prefer to have someone hold the horse, rather than tie him up.

Clippers and Blades

Our clipper blades are always sharp, and we use them with an extremely light touch. Our goal is to have them whisk through the hair and not dig or pull. We are also careful to never use the clippers if they become hot, since a hot blade against tender skin can be very uncomfortable for a horse. If he were to protest, it would be understandable.

In our program, we don't use commercial horse clippers, but rather barber clippers with an adjustable blade. This way, we don't have to stop and change blades. By moving a single lever, we can switch from a close cut (equivalent to about a size 40 with a clipper that has changeable blades) to a longer cut (about a size 10 to 15 blade). This makes it quick and easy to blend hair. The clippers we use are smaller than most horse clippers, but are dependable enough to hold up to regular use. We use two types, and we have extra pairs on hand in case one pair gets warm and we want to turn it off for a while to cool.

We use the regular sized clippers on the bridle path, face, leg and outer ear areas. For inside the ears, and the nostrils, we use another barber-type clipper that is quite small. These smaller clippers are called hair trimmers, and they have a very narrow and close cutting blade.

While we are able to purchase these clippers at beauty supply stores, you might not have such a store in your area. Ask someone at your beauty salon or barbershop where they get their clippers, and they just might help you order a pair or two from their source.

Just remember that, regardless of the type of clipper you use, clippers are not weapons. They should be held and used with a feather light grip and should float through the hair, not chug through it.

Another point to keep in mind is your horse's hair coat. For example, in the early spring or fall, if the horse hasn't been kept under lights and

1 In most cases, when a twitch is needed, we use an axe-handle type or an aluminum type (pictured here).

2 Pinching a small section of skin near the shoulder can also work as a mild restraint.

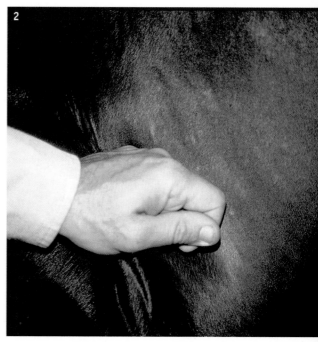

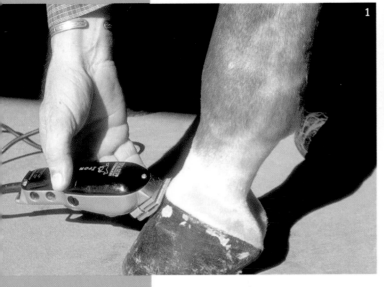

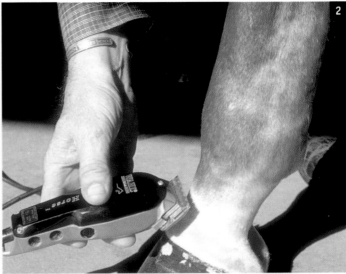

BACK-DRAGGING

The back of the leg is back-dragged, from about halfway between the back of the knee and fetlock, all the way down.

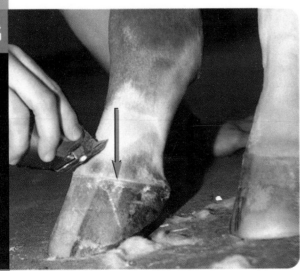

blanketed, he might be a little heavy coated. If that is the case, you will need to use a longer setting on your blades so you can blend the clipped hair and the non-clipped hair. This will keep your horse from looking like he has a poodle clip.

BACK-DRAGGING AND BLENDING: We use back-dragging in several places when clipping. back-dragging works to blend the clipped hair with the non-clipped hair that borders it, such as a white blaze with surrounding sorrel hair, or a white stocking with darker hair above it. Back-dragging is done in the opposite way you would clip if you were going against the hair.

To help understand this concept, visualize a video. In this "scene," you are clipping against the hair on a white stocking, moving upwards. You get just to the top of the white and stop. To back-drag, you just run the video backwards. Your clippers are positioned the same way, but

you are moving down instead of up, and you are working with the hair, not against it. You can have your blades set on the closest cut and won't risk gouging.

CLIPPING THE LEGS: The color of your horse's legs will determine how easy they are to clip. Dark hair, such as black, bay or chestnut, blends the easiest without showing any clipper marks. Lighter colors, such as palomino and sorrel, are more likely to show clipper marks.

With solid colored legs, we trim the hair around the coronary band with light, short, upward strokes. The blades are set on the shortest setting and are angled away from the leg to prevent cuts in the hair that are too close. Then, with the blades at a longer setting, we trim upward from the heel to the top of the fetlock indentation area. Then, the clippers are again set at their closest setting as we back-drag down through this same area.

The area behind the leg, from about halfway between the knee or hock area and to the fetlock, usually benefits from back-dragging. Also, the area around the ergot—that small bony growth behind the fetlock—can usually be smoothed with back-dragging. The same method works to smooth hair around scars.

If the horse has a white coronet band, sock or stocking, we clip the white hair. We want the hair short, but not clear down to the skin where the leg marking will appear pink instead of white. Depending on the type of clippers you use, you might have to experiment to see what setting or blade will give you the right cut. Generally, when you're clipping upwards against

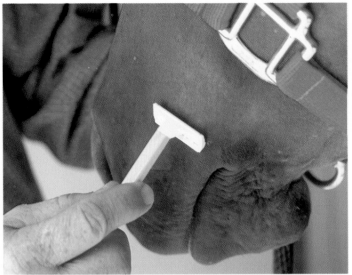

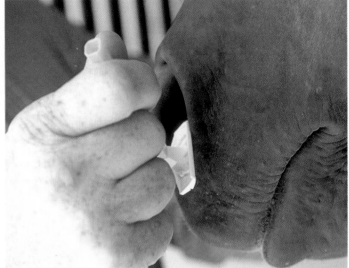

the hair, you will need the longest setting. When you get to where the white hair meets the dark, you can angle the clippers out to make a more gradual blend between the two areas.

Don't use the shortest setting when clipping against the leg hair, but use it when you're feathering up at the coronary band, or back-dragging to blend the dark and light colors.

With Paint horses that have white above the knees and hocks, we don't upward-clip the entire white area, but instead back-drag the white if the area is a little long, in order to smooth it out. We also trim around the coronary band.

CLIPPING THE MUZZLE: To remove whiskers, we use double-edged disposable razors in upward strokes. We use the razor very lightly and just on the outside of the nostrils as well as around the entire muzzle area. You can use small, narrow clippers for whisking off the hair inside the nostrils.

AROUND THE EYES: A disposable razor also works well on the long hairs above and below the eyes. With this method, you get a close cut without running the risk of jabbing a horse in the eye with a clipper blade, or making a deep clipper mark if he quickly moves his head. You can change the angle of the razor to get at the hairs.

UNDER THE JAW AND CHIN: So far, the areas we've discussed are spots that usually don't require much restraint. Clipping the jaw and chin areas won't usually bother a horse either, at least as much as the ears or bridle path. So if you

have the horse in his stall, you can slip off the halter and put it around his neck, to give you easy access for this part of the clipping.

We use our electric clippers here, setting them on the closest cut. We start at the indentation where a chin strap would rest and work upward, under the jaw. Then, the clippers are placed in a back-dragging position along the side of the jaw, on the side of the face. The hair is back-dragged in that area between the rounded jawbone to just above the mouth.

The throatlatch can also be clipped at this time by back-dragging to remove any excess hair. This technique will make the area appear much tighter.

WHITE FACE MARKINGS: For white facial markings, we use our adjustable clippers. The small clippers we use on the insides of the ears are not adjustable and, if used here, would clip too short, leaving pink skin showing where the face marking should be.

White hair usually appears thicker and longer than the dark hair that surrounds it, so it adds a wonderful, finished look when the white marking is clipped correctly.

Using the blades on the longest setting, we first clip upwards against the hair, the same way as we would on a leg. We go to the edge of the marking, then raise the blades away from the hair as we lift them away from the area. We don't want to use an against-the-hair motion on the dark hair.

Next, the clippers are positioned to that we can feather in from the sides and top, from about an inch into the dark hair, following through to

An adjustable double-edged razor can be used to trim off hairs from the muzzle area (above)

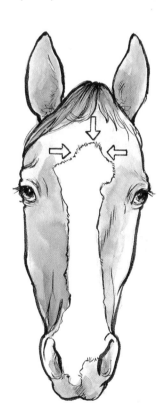

To clip face markings, after clipping upward against the hair, feather inward all along the edges the entire way around the marking.

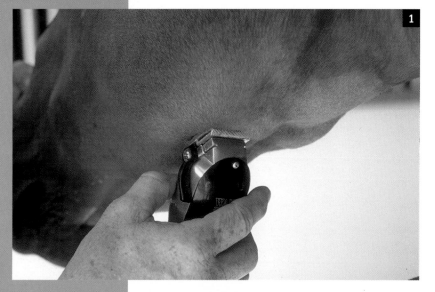

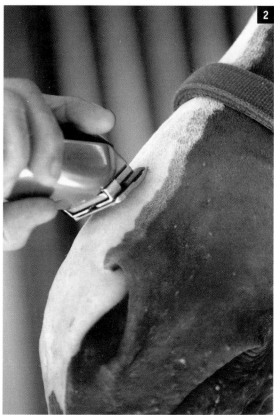

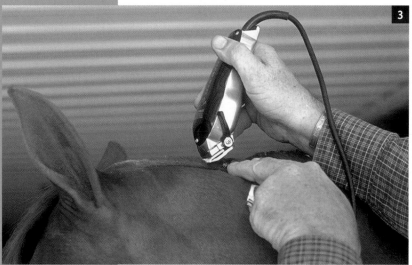

1 When clipping under the jaw, work first in an upwards motion.

2 The first step in clipping a white face marking is to move in an upward stroke against the hair.

3 To clip the bridle path, flatten the mane, and clip no more than 2 inches forward. Turn the clippers around, and clip back to the point starting point without reclipping.

the light. After this, we back-drag so to blend the dark and light hair together. This gives us a natural look, and you won't see where the clipping started or stopped.

If a horse has a real narrow white strip, we'll just touch it up by feathering in from the sides, then back-dragging down. This same method can be used with a star marking and even a bald or apron face.

CLIPPING THE BRIDLE PATH: The bridle path is a challenging area to clip. If you are not careful, you can wind up with a bridle path that is much too long. I prefer about a 4-inch-long bridle path on the babies, and about 5 inches on the older horses.

We use the clippers at the closest setting possible and clip in two separate stages. First, we hold one of our hands flat on the part of the mane that is right where the bridle path should

start. We aim the clippers forward, toward the ears. We then only clip an inch or two. If you clip in that direction too far forward, and the horse jerks his head up, you might find that you have accidentally clipping off most of your horse's forelock.

Next, we turn the clippers in the other direction, aiming back toward the mane. We start behind the point of the poll (the bump at the top of the forelock). You don't want to clip ahead of this spot. Clip back from that bump toward that first inch or two that you clipped by the mane, but don't re-clip that section.

CLIPPING THE EARS: If we know a horse will protest during this part of the clipping, we may use a twitch. Once we are ready to start, we set the clippers at the closest setting and back-drag the outside of the ear, from the base to the tip. (This only needs to be done if there are long hairs present that need to be smoothed.) We are very careful not to angle the clippers so they dig in and cause clipper marks. Those would be extremely visible in this area.

If the insides of the ears have not been clipped for quite a while, and a lot of hair is present, we use the regular clippers to whisk out the excess. We don't expect it to be perfect at this

Clipping Ears

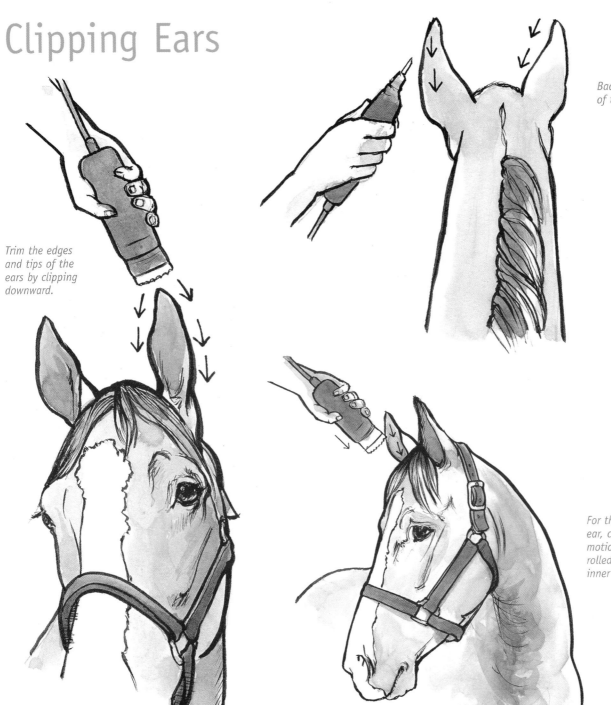

Trim the edges and tips of the ears by clipping downward.

Back-drag the outside of the ear.

For the inside of the ear, clip in a downward motion. The ear can be rolled out to help reach inner hairs.

stage. This is just a way to get part of the job done, before going in with the small hair-trimmer clippers.

After this is complete, we go inside the ear with the small, narrow hair trimmer, or ear clippers. We primarily use a downward stroke, but because some horses have hair that changes direction, the clippers might have to be angled to reach that hair.

You can roll the ear out at any time to help

the clippers reach the spot you are working on. At the flap of skin at the base of the ear, gently use your thumb to push this out so you have access to it.

After the inside of the ear is cleaned out, clip down on the outer edge, from the tip to the base, to blend.

Remember that practice makes perfect, and that your finished clipping job should look clean and natural.

Stabling at Shows

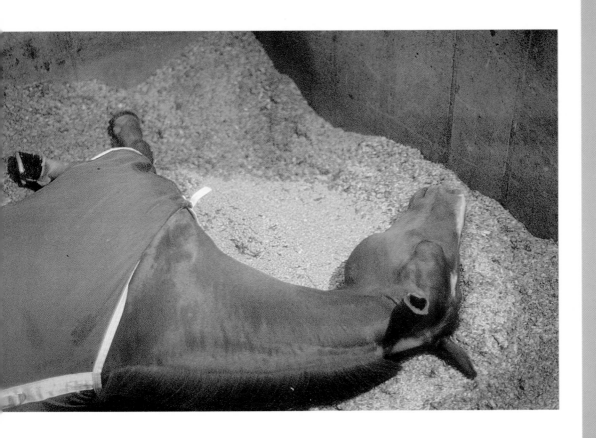

You never know what type of stalls you will have at a show until you get there. It's a good idea to take equipment and materials with you so you can alter or repair a stall as necessary.

We bring an arsenal of supplies to a show, from chains and eye-hooks, to snaps, buckets, hammers and extension cords. We are ready to make adjustments as soon as we arrive. We can use chains and large snaps to rig our feed and water buckets in each stall.

CUSTOMIZING STALLS

We mount water and feed buckets in each stall. These are stalls at the World Show.

For example, several facilities where we show have wooden partitions about 4 feet high, then wire mesh the rest of the way up. It we take two stallions to the show, we cover the wire mesh with plywood so the stallions can't see each other. We drill holes through the plywood and attach it securely with baling wire.

If we take just one stallion, our hope is that we will be stabled next to someone who has a tack stall. Then we can put the stud between their tack stall and ours.

We sometimes bring our own bagged shavings, of the same brand we use at home. If we don't bring our own, we try to buy shavings at the show that are very similar in texture and wood type to what we use at home. We have found that switching shavings can sometimes cause a horse's legs to swell.

We try to change as little as possible in the horse's housing and routine when we are at shows, especially at events like the World where so much is at stake. We haul our own alfalfa and grain. The only change we make in our normal feed program is that we take a couple of bales of hay that are a little different from what our horses usually get, such as high quality prairie hay. If a horse isn't eating his alfalfa well at the show, we give him a treat of that prairie hay, in addition to the regular alfalfa. The prairie hay is different and entices him. He will eat it and it will fill him up.

Sometimes at a lengthy show, the work routine gets off a little on the days we are actually showing. The horses we show on a certain day don't get worked. The others, who might not show for a day or two, have to be worked later in the day than they are used to. But since it's only for two or three days, it doesn't present a problem.

When showing in the colder months, we bring heat lamps that we mount high in a corner of each stall. We also bring plenty of clean stable sheets, blankets and hoods, in case we can't keep these stalls at a temperature the horses are used to. At the World, where the barns are warm, we only need to use a sheet and sheet hood on the horses to keep them at the right warmth. But, if we are at a show where the barns are cold, we use heavy blankets and hoods. We always correspond the sheets or blankets to the temperature where the horse is being stabled.

We work hard to give our horses all the comforts and consistency they get at home, regardless of where we are stabling at a show.

Before the Judging

17

When you are counting down the hours until you go to the show, the elbow grease and attention to detail you have put in start to pay off. After the horse has been clipped, it's time to bathe him.

In the warmer months, we like to bathe our horses the night before we leave for a show. Our wash rack at home has warm water with a spray nozzle on the hose. The water pressure it releases is a big help in getting white socks clean and washing shampoo out of manes and tails (which we also condition) and bodies. For the face, we use a large sponge.

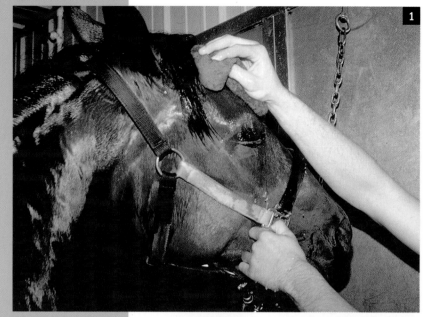

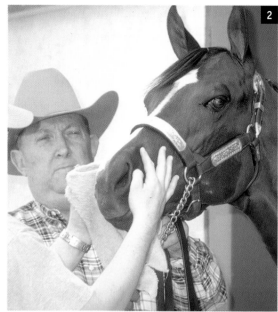

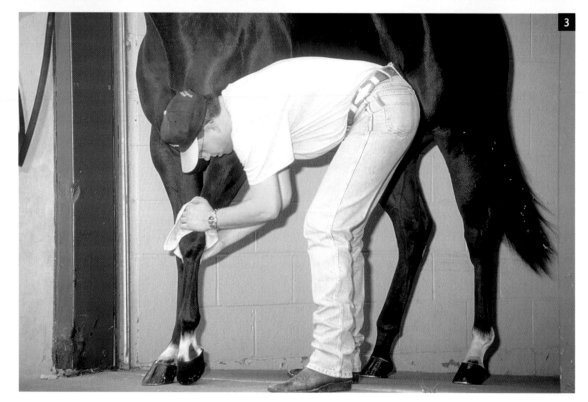

1 We bathe the horses at home, where we can use warm water.

2 Shortly before the class, we wipe out the nostrils with a soft cloth.

3 The entire horse is wiped down—body, face, neck and legs—with a clean cloth.

After rinsing out the shampoo, in order to add some shine to the body, we give the horse an oil-based rinse. This consists of ½ teaspoon of Keri Oil to each gallon of water, mixed in a bucket and sponged on the horse. We use a sweat scraper to squeeze out the excess.

In the winter, even though our barn is heated, we don't give the horses a complete bath before a show. The air is just a little too cool, even if the horses are covered while they are drying. This is when a consistent grooming and vacuuming pro-

gram really pays off. We only have to wash the white markings, then wash and condition the manes and tails. This conditioning is very effective in producing a shiny finish. After we rinse the conditioner out of the mane, we rinse it again, this time with the fresh mixture of Keri Oil and warm water. For the tail, we spray in ample amounts of a grooming product like Show Sheen and let it dry thoroughly before we comb through it.

We want to get all this "wet work" done at home, where we can use warm water. The facili-

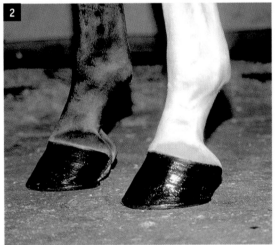

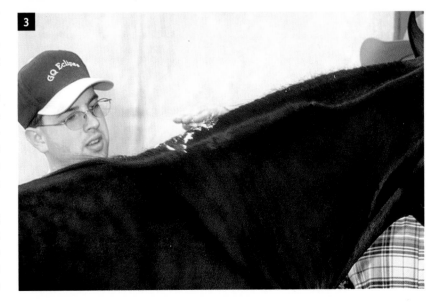

1 Hoof black is applied.

2 To produce a uniform look, we use hoof black on all feet, whether the hooves are light colored or dark. Some people prefer to use clear polish on the light colored hooves.

3 Foam mousse is applied to the banded mane to keep it flat.

ties at a show generally have only cold water and often, drafty wash racks. We don't want to subject our horses to this, so we don't bathe them at the show unless absolutely necessary. Even then, all we will do is wash white socks and markings, and that is only after we have tried to clean them by wiping the area with rubbing alcohol.

If we do have to wash the white markings, we are sure to keep the horse away from drafts while he dries. We also never wet down the body or neck; grooming and vacuuming takes care of those areas. And since our horses wear sheets or blankets and hoods at the show, their bodies and necks stay clean.

Both at home and at the show, we can work on the hooves by scrubbing them with a wire brush, or a pumice block. This not only cleans the surface, but also smooths it. Hoof black doesn't cover as nicely on a rough hoof.

As we mentioned in Chapter 8, banding wet or dry is a matter of personal preference. Whether we are stabling at a show or hauling in the morning of our classes, we like to band the night before and either straighten or re-band the next morning to be sure the mane stays down flat against the neck.

The morning of the class, we avoid getting our horses ready too soon. We don't want them standing around for long periods of time before we take them to the show pen. In fact, we rub and vacuum them, go over them with a soft

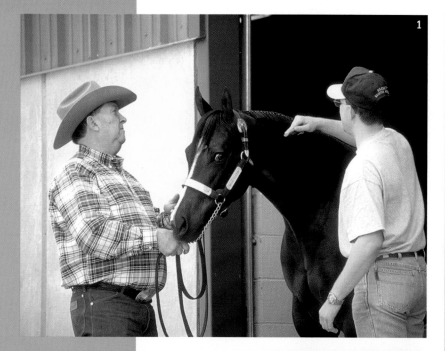

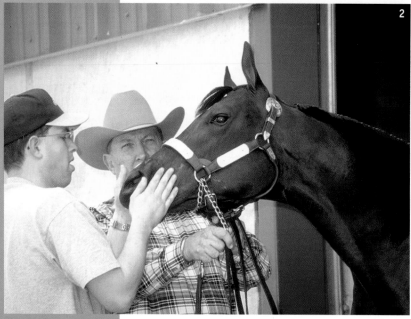

brush, then leave them alone until just before the class. We don't tie them in the hopes they will lay down and relax. Rest now helps their attitudes later, when they are in the show pen.

The final finishing before the class includes brushing the body again, combing out the tail, picking out the hooves, then applying hoof black. When we apply hoof black, we are careful to keep it even, right along the coronet band line. When you are applying hoof black, don't stroke a full dauber across the hairline, or some of the polish may bleed up into the hair. Use the full dauber on the center or bottom of the hoof. When the dauber is slightly depleted of polish,

use it near the coronet band. Keeping the hoof black even at the coronet band line is important as a hoof can look cockeyed to the judge if the hoof black is crooked.

We want everything on the horse to look uniform, which is why we use hoof black on all four feet. Some people put a clear polish on the light colored hooves, and use hoof black on the dark hooves. That is an individual preference. I like to use hoof black all the way around so everything looks the same.

When we work on the manes and tails, we comb out the tail and apply a foam mousse to the top to flatten it on the top and sides. We also put mousse on the banded manes. If quite a bit of excess mousse was applied, we gently blot it with a towel. Most of it will evaporate, however.

If a horse has a thick forelock, it helps to put one band in the forelock. This keeps it from looking unruly, or fanning out all over the forehead.

Next, we use a soft rag to clean out the nostrils and, if needed, the insides of the ears. We also keep a small, disposable razor handy to shave any whiskers on the muzzle that might have been missed during clipping.

We use fly spray only on the legs and belly before going into a class, but not on the body. If applied to the body when a horse is being shown outdoors and standing in the sun, the spray

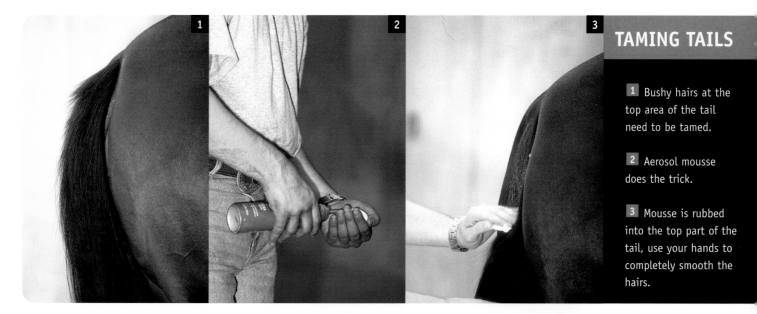

TAMING TAILS

1 Bushy hairs at the top area of the tail need to be tamed.

2 Aerosol mousse does the trick.

3 Mousse is rubbed into the top part of the tail, use your hands to completely smooth the hairs.

causes the hair to stand up. If a horse really needs protection from flies, we use a coat conditioning spray. However, that too can cause the hair to rise.

We put the show halter on before we oil the face. We do this so oil isn't picked up off the face and absorbed into the underside of the web stable halter. We use oil generously around the eyes and all over the muzzle. We are careful not to get any oil from our hands on the leather of the lead shank. An oily lead shank can slide right through your hands.

A cooler is put on the horse to keep his hair flat while we lead him to the show pen. We have two weights of coolers; the one we choose depends on the air temperature the horse will be exposed to while waiting in the wings. Our lightweight coolers are satin on the outside, with a taffeta liner. The heavyweight coolers are of this same general construction, but have a foam center, like a coat. The non-abrasive slickness of the taffeta lining really shines the hair.

Just before the horse goes into the show pen, we remove his cooler by pulling it off straight back, so it encourages the hair to stay down. Pulling it off to the side causes the hair to ruffle.

All this attention to detail ultimately pays off.

The tail is combed out.

Show Pen Strategy

18

S uccessfully showing at halter is a frame of mind. You take an attitude with you when you enter the pen. You know it, your horse knows it and the judge knows it. Your personality and the way you walk, dress and present yourself should exude so much charisma that you pack a lot of clout.

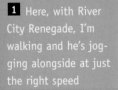

1 Here, with River City Renegade, I'm walking and he's jogging alongside at just the right speed

2 If the arena dirt is quite deep and your horse's toes are way down, but his heels are up, his pasterns will appear too upright. This will give his hocks the appearance of having too much set.

3 In this deep dirt, one foot is set lower than the other. This destroys the overall look of balance that you strive to achieve.

4 You can smooth some dirt with your foot or just move a short distance to a place where the dirt is more packed. This gives you a better chance of property placing the horse's feet.

From the second you enter the pen, your mind must be totally committed to doing a good job of showing that horse. Your concentration must be finely tuned so that at all times, you know what your horse is doing and where the judges are. Someone could yell, "Fire!" but would have to yell it twice to get your attention. While everyone else was stampeding out the gate, you would still have your mind set on presenting that horse the best way you know how.

It takes practice to become this confident and focused. If you make mistakes when you first begin showing horses, claim them not as errors, but as happy accidents that will help you learn from what you did wrong. If you are having problems, get someone to shoot a video of your class. Also have them shoot a tape of either a top trainer, or someone who consistently beats you in your youth or amateur classes. Study those videos and see the techniques being used.

Compare your horse's fitness with the fitness of the others. Watch how the handler sets up his horse and how he moves to give the judge the best look. Check out the person's dress and demeanor. If you are going to beat him someday, you have to find out why he is beating you now.

It will also help to absorb the following information:

When you lead your horse in, stay right beside him, at his head, with your arm at his throatlatch. Don't pull his head toward you; doing so might cause him to move sideways. If he jumps or plays, you can take hold of him and back him a few steps, then start again. Remember: the judges know these horses are fit, high and playful. They aren't surprised when they see a halter horse jump or play, especially when it is jogged out.

At one time, halter horses were moved out at a fast clip, but now a pleasure horse jog is called for. A handler can usually walk, and have the horse jog alongside of him. When it's your turn, you can choose the jog speed that shows your horse best. If he is moving at a crawl and it

appears that he is still walking, pick up the pace just a little, but remember: you want a jog.

At Quarter Horse shows, you will be asked to pass the judge and trot off to the side, sometimes around a cone. If your horse is sore, he is going to show it when he makes that turn. If he is not sore, you sure don't want pilot error to make him look like he is. Mistakes here can make even the soundest horse look lame. Most of the time, you will move off to the left. I never make a sharp 90-degree turn when I do this; I make a round turn. That way, I can execute it without pulling on the horse's head. If you jerk the shank down and out to force a tight turn, the horse's head will shoot up. This interferes with his stride and makes him appear lame.

It's really tough when the judge has you turn off to the right and push the horse away from you. Again, I make a round turn and do it without pulling on the shank. I lift my right hand so the chain isn't down, and I use my knuckles to push the horse's jaw. This makes him move his head away.

Your horse might be confused about turning in this direction, so you may want to take a slight hold of him before you start the round turn to the right. This will slow him down a little, but you can give him back his head as you make the turn, and help him pick up his pace afterwards. Next, you will be heading for the lineup.

You can practice this at home by setting up a cone at the spot where you would make that 90-degree round turn. Without overdoing it to the point that the horse automatically starts cutting a corner when he sees a cone, you can prac-

tice until you and your horse are comfortable with this move.

At most shows, the horses are placed in a head-and-tail line to be judged. At the smaller weekend shows, one line is usually asked for, and you can call the shots as to the order that you enter the ring. This is not done on a draw. If enough horses are present to form two lines, and you can choose which line you want to be in, think about which side the judges will be on when they walk up and down to compare the horses in the profiling. You can use this to your advantage.

For example, if you banded your horse's mane to minimize a cresty or ewe-neck, the mane side will give the best profile view, presenting what appears to be a more perfect neck.

Face markings also make a difference. If I have a horse who has a lot of white on one side of his face, such as an apron face, but is fairly solid on the other, I like to show the solid side to the judge as he checks profiles—assuming the rest of the horse also presents a better picture from that side.

Once you have chosen your place in line, be sure you and your horse are beyond kicking distance from the horse in front you. And, leave plenty of room for the judge to walk safely around behind.

Set up your horse while taking arena conditions into consideration. If the dirt is quite deep and your horse's toes are way down into it, but his heels are up, it's going make his pasterns look too upright. His hocks will also appear to have too much set.

1 Keeping a horse's head in a natural position, but one that still shows charisma, will enhance his overall profile.

2 This is a 2-year-old stallion who is showing well as I keep a little distance from his head.

In this shot, I'm keeping the horse in the correct and alert position as he's being judged.

If you can smooth some dirt with your foot, or move a short distance to a place where the dirt is more packed, you have a better chance of getting things right. (See photos on page 110.)

Sometimes, you will have to hand-place a back foot. Be sure to do it without pulling on the horse's head and causing him to move. Some horses will automatically move their hindquarters away from you as soon as you step to the back, so if you can set the back feet only by maneuvering the lead shank, be sure to choose that option.

If the horse has a back foot in the right position, but has the foot cocked, don't walk toward his hindquarters and push his hip or pull his tail to rock his weight back onto that foot. Instead, just stay in front of him. With your toe, tap the front foot on the same side as the one in the rear that is cocked. The horse will set the back foot down.

When you are working on the front feet and you have to hand-place one, be sure to do it in time to be set up when the judge gets to you. At the World, in the yearling stallion class with Pure Play, I quickly hand-placed a foot because the judges were coming right down the line. Pure Play was the second horse they would look at. I didn't have time to work off his head to get him right.

At smaller shows, I advise my amateurs to leave well enough alone if the judge is right there, and the horse is set up close to being cor-

rect but is not perfect. A judge will give you a few moments to get things right, but if a foot is only an inch or two off, it looks unprofessional to struggle repeatedly to correct such a small error right in front of the judge.

If you are a fairly green exhibitor and aren't sure if you tend to set up your horse too far under or spread way out, you might want to have a hand signal system worked out with someone along the rail so they can help you. Let this person know just how you want to set up your horse. If you are off, your rail helper can give you a signal.

How your horse is put together should effect your decision on how to set him up. If he's a little weak in the back, don't stand him stretched out. Doing so will drop his topline and make his back look even weaker. Bring his hind legs up under him a little more and set him closer.

A sickle-hocked horse has hocks that naturally come way out behind him. Set him up so he is under himself. You want the point of his hocks directly below the point of his buttocks.

The opposite holds true for the horse whose hocks are set way up under him. Stretch this horse out just a little, but not so far that his hocks are out behind his buttocks area. You don't want to show a horse that has been set up to look like he is camped up under himself.

A "posty-hocked" horse—one that is set straight up and down—should stand with his legs positioned naturally.

When you know things are right with the way you have set your horse, start thinking about getting his head in position and about keeping his attention.

If his head gets too high, his topline will sag and his neck will look funny. A low head will cause the neck to look too deep underneath in the area where it ties into the chest. This can ruin a horse's profile.

The more natural the position the better, as long as his head and neck stay put and he shows some charisma while the judge is looking at him.

When you're presenting your horse well, it is easy to give a confident smile to the judge when he walks around to take a look. During this time, you will also need to know how to keep your horse's attention and expression.

To accomplish this, you must be able to read your horse and be very aware that his age and experience are factors to consider.

The perfect expression is one of fascination

and interest, like a horse that is out in a field and sees a dog running across it. The horse will stiffen up and really give you what we call "The Look."

Some horses won't give you The Look if you stand too close to them. As you stand with your feet at a three-quarter angle to the horse, you might have to step back if you see your horse pinning his ears or otherwise acting annoyed at your closeness. As you back off a little, you might see his ears come up. And, hopefully, he will reach with his neck, and his eyes will brighten. Some older or seasoned horses will reliably act this way. But unseasoned horses might move if you back away too far.

When you are showing weanlings, stay close to their heads to give them confidence and keep them from getting scared. The newness of their surroundings is usually enough to get a look out of them. Keep them looking straight ahead and don't let them gawk.

If a horse of any age turns his head and loses that straight-ahead position, poke your finger through the halter ring to push his head back where it should be. In fact, push him a little beyond where he should be. When you remove your finger, he'll put his head right where you want it. This method is described in more detail in Chapter 12.

Some horses need incentive to give you their ears and show that nice expression. If you have schooled your horse at home to show expression as you double the end of your lead shank and lightly tap him between the eyes, he will react to the sound of the leather snapping. Then, in the show pen, all you have to do is move the shank toward his forehead and pull it away. He will give you the expression you want as he watches it.

You might also try carrying a small stash of grain or alfalfa in the same hand that will hold the leather end of the lead shank. Let your horse smell it, then pull it away. He will stretch to reach it.

When you are after that stretch and expression, you want to time it so you are sure it will be there when the judge is two horses away from looking at you. Hold that expression until the judge has looked at your horse and moved on to the next.

Expect some frustrating times in the show pen. Some horses are just not going to give you their ears as part of the expression package. With a horse like this, if you only get the exten-

PHOTO COURTESY OF THE QUARTER HORSE JOURNAL

It all pays off. This is Mister GQ when we were about to accept his trophy as World Champion Aged Stallion.

sion of the head and neck, don't worry about the ears. If you pick on him because you are frustrated, matters will just get worse. Instead of that charismatic look, you'll get a dirty look instead. You don't want to create an unpleasant expression.

Regardless of what happens, keep a positive attitude and show it to the judge. Keep showing your horse until the judge turns in that scorecard. Just remember that some horses are easy to show because they have that natural show horse attitude and are full of "want-to." Others don't enjoy it. Read your horse and do the best job you can with what you have.

Looking Back

I have had the privilege of showing many wonderful halter horses over the years. This chapter highlights just a few of them.

One of the really terrific aspects of this business is showing a top young stallion, then having the opportunity to show his get when he proves himself as a sire. This has happened with three of the horses profiled here, and started when I showed Conclusive. A few years later, I showed his grandson, Kid Clu, then Kid's son, River City Renegade. It didn't stop there. I have also shown a number of Renegade's sons and daughters.

When Mister GQ won the Quarter Horse World in aged stallions, I already had some of his get in my barn, including GQ Silhouette and GQ Eclipse. Now, I'm leading several Eclipse babies and look forward to the time when they, too, will fill my barn with winners.

▼ Conclusive

Conclusive, who is by Impressive, was a weanling when he came into my barn. One of my clients purchased him from us after we had picked him out at 3 months old. Even at that young age, he had the look of being a great one. He got better and better every day after he was weaned. I could see the future in him. I showed him until he was 16 months old; then Jerry Wells of Purcell, Oklahoma, purchased him. Jerry won the World with Conclusive when the horse was a 4-year-old. The horse went on to sire such greats as Mr Conclusion and Obvious Conclusion.

▶ Kid Clu

A grandson of Conclusive, Kid Clu was sired by Obvious Conclusion. I led Kid Clu when he was a 2-year-old, and again at 3, at the World. He was a pleasure to work with, and was very intelligent, kind and willing to learn. His personality was terrific. He also had the most awesome front end I've ever seen on a horse, and was just great overall. He fit together everywhere: the front end, back end and top line. He was a fabulous individual who really stood out in the show pen. Kid Clu was full of ring presence and show-horse attitude. Wherever he went, he drew a crowd. When he came out of the pen, people would swarm around him.

PHOTO COURTESY OF DON SHUGART

HAROLD COMPTON

◀ Spanish Array

Spanish Array was a great horse to show because he had so much expression, and his coat shone like copper in the pen. He was the biggest-hipped horse I have ever seen and was a great individual to boot. The late Hank Weiscamp was the breeder of this horse.

This stallion was 5 when he came to our barn. He had been shown as a 3-year-old by Margaret Hammond, of Peyton, Colorado. In 1985, I won the Quarter Horse World with him. This was just a wonderful horse to be around. He was super kind. We really loved handling him.

Robert Haas of Indiana bought Spanish Array when the horse was in his teens. The horse that Charlie Dobbs won the Quarter Horse Congress with in 1996 was sired by Spanish Array. That same horse, in the same year, also won the Youth World.

◀ Ladys Flower

This mare earned more than 1,000 halter points, and Lester Flanders showed her to a lot of them. I won the Quarter Horse World with her in 1983, when she was a 2-year-old. She was Honor Roll mare more than once, and was truly a great one. She was built a lot like Kid Clu and balanced like him, and also like River City Renegade. She was eventually sold to someone in Brazil as a brood-mare.

◀ Mr Joe Will

Mr Joe Will was a chestnut with a lot of chrome and had an absolutely awesome front end. If his head had been any prettier, there would not have been a stallion or gelding in the country that could have beat him. It was tough to get his ears up in the show pen, and if you didn't get them, his head was really a contrast to his terrific body.

He was a fun horse to be around because he was a comedian. He would suck on his tongue and doodle around all the time, keeping us entertained. Not only did he have a wonderful personality, but he was very kind.

Harold
Campton

▲ River City Renegade

This son of Kid Clu had the same quality and charisma as his daddy. I looked at Renegade for the first time when he was just 4 days old. He really had The Look.

Renegade came into our barn as a weanling and was here until he left for the breeding season of his 2-year-old year. The day after he bred the last of more than 25 mares, he came back to our barn. You would never know this stallion had been used for breeding because he was so easy to get along with. Renegade has so many of his sire's traits, including the wonderful personality.

Renegade was always a real character. When we worked him in the pen, he would grab the longe line and swing his head and play. We never got after him because he was just having a good time. He was one of those horses who loved everything he did.

In 1996, Lowell Stewart of Stewart Quarter Horses in Lawrence, Kansas, won the Amateur 2-Year-Old Stallion class at the World with Renegade. Two of our crew, Ruth Murphy and Aaron Hall, were standing outside the gate watching. They both jumped and shouted with tears streaming down their faces when Renegade won. They truly loved this horse.

A few days later, I led Renegade in the open 2-year-old stallion class and he was Reserve Champion. After the World, he went home to Lawrence, Kansas, where his first baby, a filly, arrived seven weeks later.

COURTESY OF THE QUARTER HORSE JOURNAL

◀ Mister GQ

In 1996, I led Mister GQ to win the Aged Stallion class at the Quarter Horse World. He is a son of Mr Conclusive. Ted Turner of Aubrey, Texas, had previously shown him, winning the Congress the year before. His owner, Candace Jussen of Pilot Point, Texas, had won the World with him in the amateur class when he was a yearling.

Mister GQ had wonderful overall balance and was very pretty headed. And, he wasn't just a halter horse. He was started under saddle and the horse earned a number of riding points. In fact, I judged him when Candace rode him at the Solid Gold. He was a big time loper. He was just a gorgeous horse under saddle.

A few weeks after I led him to the Aged Stallion win at the World, I showed his son, GQ Eclipse, in his debut as a yearling stallion at the Denver Stock Show. He stood first under five of the six judges and won a grand and two reserves. He had been in our fitting program less than a month. Like his daddy, he is just an outstanding individual.

PHOTO COURTESY OF HAROLD COMPTON

Harold
Compton

▲ **Lady Bens Impression**

This mare won both the Quarter Horse Congress and the
World. She was Honor Roll filly as a yearling, which was
the year she came to my barn. She was the type of horse
you could look at standing in a stall and just know she
was a good one. When she went in the show pen, you
could see she was an exceptional horse. When she was in
her show clothes, she was really fancy. She would just
show her heart out.

She eventually left our barn and was still shown for a
while. She eventually became a broodmare and was bred
to Obvious Conclusion. She later died at the breeding
farm after delivering his foal. It's tough to lose those
great ones.

◄ St High Society

It's hard to recognize great show horses in the halter industry without paying tribute to the wonderful brood-mares that produce them. One mare that graced our pasture for many years produced foals that grew to earn a total of 1,332 AQHA points. A mare belonging to Leslie Woolley of Wichita, Kansas, St High Society, is recognized as one of the all time AQHA leading halter dams for Open, Amateur and Youth halter horses. Leslie purchased this 1979 mare as a 2-year-old, so it was particularly gratifying for her to watch the mare's offspring do so well over the years.

Nicknamed "Slide," St High Society was sired by AQHA Champion and Superior Halter Horse Slide Me Five. Her dam is a granddaughter of Tonto Bars Dude.

The dam of 12 foals, Slide produced 10 World Qualifiers. We started the show careers of seven of those horses: Ovations; River City Rolex; Astentatious; The Power To Impress; Endorsements; High Continuitee; and Kidding Me.

Slide produced one World Champion, three Reserve World Champions (with seven Championships among them), seven World Show Top 10 horses that stood in that bracket 31 times, 10 Superior Halter horses, and a total of 25 Register Of Merits earned. One of Slide's offspring was an AQHA High Point Halter Horse. One earned a Top 10 place in the Justin Rookie of the Year placings.

At 20 years of age, Slide foaled Ovations, her black filly by GQ Eclipse. Like many of Slide's foals, this filly didn't have a real mature look as a weanling. Most of Slide's previous babies grew tall and slender until about the middle of their 2-year-old year, or even until the first of their 3-year-old year. Then, they would start to bulk up and just get better and better. They just needed that extra time to mature. We knew we would have to give this black filly some time to show that maturity, so we didn't take her to the World as a baby.

We were right, and by her 2-year-old year, the filly had put on a lot of natural bulk. She did well at the World when I showed her in the Open, and also when Leslie showed her in Amateur.

Slide is truly one of those great broodmares.

WM. J. STINSON

W ith both eyes open, young Denny Hassett learned to ride on a one-

eyed pony in his hometown of Tonganoxie, Kansas. It wasn't

because he wanted to. He didn't care much about horses or ponies

back then. For his family, getting Denny to ride was like trying to

force broccoli down the throat of a pre-schooler.

"I remember when I was real small, we'd go to a country fair

show and my sister would ride in the potato races and musical

chairs," Denny recalls. "Once in a while, they'd get me to take in my

little one-eyed pony, but I wasn't much in favor it."

Denny says he didn't have anything against horses and the activities they performed. But at the time, he just wasn't interested. After all, his father drove teams and farmed with work horses. Horses were just always around, like tractors, cars or pickup trucks.

Of course, none of these motorized vehicles were as tall as those big, wide draft horses that weighed in at close to 1,500 pounds. Denny's father not only farmed with these horses, but also spent 13 years competing in pulling contests, all the time patiently wondering when his son would finally take the reins.

In the early 1960s, when Denny was 22, something clicked. "My dad had a real good friend named George Wingate," Denny says. "He had a son just a year younger than me who would go to open shows and ride reiners. I'd go with them once in a while, just to watch. I decided I wanted to try it. That's how I finally got involved."

At this point, Denny still lived in northeast Kansas. Tonganoxie was just 35 miles west of Kansas City. At the time Denny took up an interest in horses, many open and saddle club shows were active in the area. Besides attending these shows with the Wingates, Denny also went with another friend, Bo Freeman.

Pleased as punch, Denny's father presented Denny with a grey mare who was sired by a Quarter Horse stud out of one of the work horse mares.

"He gave her to me when I was 22," Denny says, "and she was the horse I started on."

Denny schooled the mare as a reiner and took her to open shows. Soon, he bought other horses. "I got really serious about the reining," he says.

For a few years, Denny divided his time between his reining horse hobby and a job at the gas company. But because of his success in the show pen, people kept calling, trying to get him to ride their horses. In 1970, he kissed the gas company job goodbye and went to full-time training. Soon, he was riding Quarter Horses, Appaloosas and Paints at open shows. Most of his customers owned Quarter Horses, so before long, he was attending a number of Quarter Horse-only shows. He gradually branched out from just riding reiners to what he calls "everything."

Those were the Quarter Horse days of roached manes, and tails that were shortened just above the hocks. And, Denny says, "If your horse was fat, pretty and slick, you could rinse away the sweat after you rode him, dry him off and halter him."

Before long, Denny had a partner in this operation. In 1972, he married Dana Sullivan, who showed some of his horses in English, western pleasure and trail. In 1978, they moved to western Kansas, where they fit and showed such top halter horses as Conclusive, Impressive Dandy and six-time World Champion Decker Impressive. Dana continued to show some of the riders until the mid-80s, when she was sidelined by a horse-related accident.

At the time that Dana was helping out with the riding, the Hassett's barn had every thing from reiners and railers to halter horses. But in 1989, the year the couple moved to the Wichita, Kansas, area, Denny decided he had to go one way or the other: halter or performance. He chose to spend the rest of his career specializing in fitting and showing halter horses.

"I'd always liked the big, pretty halter horses, and really enjoyed fitting them and seeing the potential," he says. "I liked the riding part, too, but because of my age and the demands of doing both performance and halter, I knew I couldn't keep doing both."

At that time, it wasn't unusual for a trainer to show his halter horses first thing, then show the riders until 2 or 3 the next morning. Then, Denny says, "You started it all again at 7 a.m."

During the time Denny was working this gruelling schedule, he was racking up wins. He won the Quarter Horse Congress in reining with a horse called Jet Fleet, a AAA son of Jet Deck, out of an Otoe mare. He also won in reining at the Congress on a mare called Handdown Socks.

A sorrel stud, Peppy Boy Too, carried Denny to a scored place in the 2-year-old Congress Western Pleasure Futurity, then placed second in Congress pleasure classes for the next year. Later, the horse won the Congress Versatility.

When Denny made the decision to bow out from showing performance horses, he went out with a bang. "When I moved to the Wichita area," he recalls, "I had a horse called Buck The Vantage. I was ninth on him at the World in Junior Pleasure. That was the last time I ever rode a pleasure horse. The last reiner I rode was Handdown Socks. She was Reserve World Champion behind Al Dunning and Expensive Hobby."

All this time, he'd also had halter horses in his barn and now they were being joined by more: champions such as Kid Clu, Hollys Payday, Mr. Joe Will and Can't Stop Stylin. In less than a decade of specializing, Denny had accumulated scores of American Quarter Horse Association and American Paint Horse Association World and Reserve World Champions, as well as a Palomino World Champion. Many of the youth and amateur horses he'd trained and fit also won a number of Youth World Championships and Reserves.

In 1995, Denny and Dana moved to rural Burns, Kansas, northeast of Wichita. Situated on 45 serene acres of grassy, rolling hills, their place is an ideal horse environment and a beautiful inspiration for Dana's artwork. She is an accomplished painter who often looks out at the broodmares grazing near the pond, a sight that encourages her to include the familiar in many of her impressionistic oils.

The ranch's contemporary house and top-notch show barn attest to the success Denny has enjoyed in the horse business. The barn has consistently been full of World and Congress winners.

The kid who once had to be forced to ride a one-eyed pony has come a long way.

GAIL BATES

Lynda Bloom Layne has owned horses of several breeds since the mid-1950s. She showed many of them to regional and state year-end high point titles, in halter and performance. Some of the Paints she raised have shown successfully at the World and Congress levels.

In 1967, Layne's first article was published in *Appaloosa News* (now *Appaloosa Journal*), thus beginning her career as a writer. She has written more than 1,000 articles for equine and other magazines to date.

Layne's previous books include *Fitting & Showing the Halter Horse* and *Horse of Course! Guide to Winning the Western Trail Class*, both published in 1980. Her first novel, *Silent Scream*, was released in 2001. She is currently working on a second novel.

Lynda describes herself as a single mother of two small, spoiled dogs; one equally spoiled Paint filly; and a cat with an attitude. She currently lives in the Pacific Northwest.

Page numbers in *italic* indicate illustrations.